Good Grief
For Hurting Hearts

By

Apostle Eugene Satterwhite Th.D.

© 2002 by Apostle Eugene Satterwhite Th.D.
All rights reserved.

No part of this book may be reproduced, stored in a retrieval system, or transmitted by any means, electronic, mechanical, photocopying, recording, or otherwise, without written permission from the author.

ISBN: 0-7596-6639-3 (e-book)
ISBN: 0-7596-6640-7 (Paperback)

This book is printed on acid free paper.

Cover Photography Copyright © 1997 by Morris Press

Published by: Divine Life Publications
P.O. Box 31099 • Capitol Heights, MD 20731 • (301) 218-9085
www.divinelifeworship.org

Printed in the United States by Morris Publishing
3212 East Highway 30
Kearney, NE 68847

1stBooks – rev. 03/25/03

Featuring Medical, Scientific, Psychological, and Biblical Principles For overcoming Grief and Loss

Dr. Apostle Eugene Satterwhite, TH.D.

This book is dedicated to the memory of my son
Jerome Allen Satterwhite and my mother
Lillian Satterwhite
And to the victims and families
of the September 11th tragedy

Acknowledgements

There were many people who played an important role in my life to help make me the man of God I am today. These are but a few:

Evangelist Joy Satterwhite - My wife and best friend

The late Bishop E.F. Morris - Founder and pastor of Gods Pentecostal Church and the Full Gospel Association. He was one of the wisest men I've ever met.

Pastor Dr. Edna Travis - Pastor and founder of New Covenant Pentecostal Tabernacle and The United Interdenominational Fellowship. She was my pastor, counselor, and friend.

The late Pastor Pearl Williams - Pastor and founder of House of Prayer Full Gospel Pentecostal Church. They called her the songbird of the Northwest. She taught me how to hold a note and keep a song in my heart.

The late Bishop Willie Jackson - Pastor of South Side Temple. He was there for me. He helped me buy my first car.

The late Dr. Theresa Martin - Founder of Divine Trinity Full Gospel Church and Rise and Be Healed Ministries. I was saved under her dynamic ministry.

Bishop A. A. Wells - Pastor and founder of Emmanuel Temple and President of the Full Gospel Pentecostal Association. He taught me integrity. It was a pleasure to serve under such a great leader.

Pastor J. L. and Willie Vaughn - Pastor of Salvation Inn for All Nations. They were my spiritual parents who never gave up on me.

Evangelist Cassie McCain - A real prayer warrior who helped me pray through many times.

Bishop Dr A. L. Hardy - Pastor of Rose of Sharon and Founder of the A. L. Hardy Academy of the Bible. He is my teacher and mentor. He had faith in me and inspired me to higher education.

Mother Rachel Procter - Pastor of New Life Holiness Church. She pushed me toward excellence, teaching me who I am in God.

Mother Stella Boyd - It was this powerful mother's prayer that lifted me from the negative grief and birthed in me the praise and worship songs.

Owen Satterwhite - My dad and friend. He always worked hard to provide the best that he could for us.

Mother Hannah Jones and Family

The Lormis Family

Elder Arthur Howie

The Moore Family

The Curlin Family

The Shekinah Glory and Lovinac Family

Evangelist Machelle Wall - Special Thanks

Theresa Setoodeh – Special Thanks

Bobbie Richardson

Table of Contents

Foreword xi
From Shock To Reality 1
Erase It, Trace It, Or Face It 7
Just When I thought Things Couldn't Get Worse 12
Why Me, Lord? 24
The Results Of A Bad Decision 26
The Physical, Mental, and Spiritual Aspects of Grief 33
The Rejected Reject 43
Pass the Grief 48
The Love Connection 52
Who's To Blame 57
The Woman Thou Gaveth Me 63
Overcoming "Triple A" (Anger, Attitude, and Anxiety) 67
Living With Losses and Loving Life 72
Handicapped By Hopelessness 77
When Mamas Go Home 87
Heaven In My View 110
I Have A Dream, But It's A Set Up 115
It's Not Over Till It's Over 119
Breaking The Cycle 127
Gaining Record Breaking Victory from Past Mistakes 131
Facing Tomorrow 135
Let There Be Light 139

Foreword

If there is any subject in the world my wife and I feel comfortably qualified to expound on, it is grief and loss. Though we don't claim to have all the answers on this timely subject, our lives are a testimony of God's power to sustain one in their darkest hour, when hope seems hopeless and dreams are shattered, when everything you've trusted in seems to have failed, and there's no visual chance of change. We feel favored by God to share with you some of our life threatening experiences that you also may have hope as well.

After being married several years, I thought life was just grand. I was the pastor of a slow growing church, but we were all happy. Devastation hit us like a ton of bricks. I felt like Job's twin. I kept wondering, why me? In one year we suffered through the brutal murder of our second born son, our marriage was shaken, our ministry nearly destroyed and most of all, rejected from those we loved and trusted down through the years. Through all of this God's hand of mercy was still upon us. I believe everything we suffer is for a purpose. I used to think what we suffered was all for our own good. The Bible says, in *Isaiah 53:15, "He was wounded for our transgressions, bruised for our iniquities, and the chastisement of our peace was upon him."* Therefore, we find everything Christ suffered was for us. To be like Christ our suffering should be beneficial to others. If our suffering can make life easier for someone else, then our suffering has not been in vain. In *Isaiah 53:3*, it says, *"He is despised and rejected of men; A man of sorrows and acquainted with grief..."* Jesus is acquainted with grief. Therefore he can relate to our pain and suffering. Jesus faced grief and loss like we do. He expressed sorrow at the loss of his fellow minister, John the Baptist. He wept at the grave sight of his dear friend, Lazarus. In *St. Matthew 26:38*, Jesus said to his disciple: *"My soul is exceedingly sorrowful, even unto death; tarry ye here, and watch with me."* Every human being on the face of this earth is subject to grief and loss, no one is exempt. Grief and loss don't mean give up and lose. It can be taken as predator or prey, medicine or poison, therapeutic or physically traumatizing, depending on how it is channeled. Although many books have been written on grief, and psychiatrists and counselors have tried to outline basic guidelines of what a person is supposed to experience, no one can really know the true feelings of one's soul but one's self. As a pastor, I had to go back and apologize to a few people I had ministered to, who had lost a loved one. I'd tell them, "I know what you are going through. I feel your pain." I was wrong, I didn't know. I soon found out the enlightening truth that some things in life can only truly be known by experience.

The intense pain I felt after learning of my son's death, was like nothing I had ever experienced. Although much needed, words of encouragement sounded like brass and a tinkling symbol. Medicine was to no avail. Close friends and loved ones would often make me feel like a zombie or an alien from another planet. When I walked in the room, I was the focus of everyone's attention. They'd look at me as if I were an AIDS patient and was about to die at any moment. One well trusted woman even asked me to sign for some money she was giving to me. She heard people who are grieving lose their memory. I would also be further confused with mixed messages like, "Let go, hold on, don't cry, cry it all out, try to stay busy, you need your rest, talk to someone, don't talk until you are ready." I soon began to accept the harsh reality that many of them didn't really know what I was going through, or how to minister to me. Although they meant well, they were just applying what they had heard, not realizing every case is different. May this book serve as a message of hope for those who have or are experiencing grief and for those with hurting hearts.

Dr. Apostle Eugene Satterwhite

From Shock To Reality

It was Sunday, February 19, 1989. Our morning worship service had just ended. I had recently completed the longest fast I had ever endeavored, 31 days, so I didn't preach the message that morning. My wife and I were downstairs preparing dinner for the feeding program for the poor and homeless people that often hung around the church. Two young men came and asked to speak with us. We stepped to the side and they informed us our son had been shot. In our panic- stricken state, we dropped everything and headed for our son's apartment. We left so fast we didn't even ask which son had been shot, Micah or Jerome. Micah is the oldest and it was his apartment, so we assumed it was Micah. When we arrived at the apartment we were told that Jerome was taken to the hospital with a gunshot wound to the head. We left immediately for the hospital. When we arrived one of the nurses took us to a little private room and told us the doctor wanted to see us, but he needed a chaplain present. My heart seemed to have sunk down to my stomach. I felt sick inside as a hopeless, helpless feeling seemed to have taken complete possession of me. Dozens of questions crossed my mind. Why do we need a chaplain? What words are going to come from the lips of this doctor that would merit the presence of a chaplain? "My son is not going to die," I kept telling myself. I've known several people who had gotten shot in the head and still lived through it. God would not allow this to happen to such a nice family like ours, so I thought. He is too loving and kind to do this to me.

The ten or fifteen minutes it took for the doctor and the chaplain to come in seemed like ten or fifteen hours. The chaplain came in first. They sent a female chaplain. She was kind and very sensitive, but she would not give us any information about our son until the doctor came in. When the doctor finally came in he wasn't as nice. He was firm, to the point, and in my opinion not so sensitive. He said, "Your son's condition is quite critical, and he probably won't live through this. Although he's not brain dead, there's severe irreparable brain damage." After a period of pain filled tearful questions and answers with the doctor, he said, "You have some very hard decisions to make. First of all, you must decide if you want us to go in and operate. There's not much we can do except clean up the wounds a bit. I really don't think we should bother. If he does, by some miraculous means, live through this, he'll be a complete vegetable. If it were my own son I would let whatever happens, happen. Then, you must decide if he stops breathing and functioning on his own, do you want us to try to revive him and put him on life support because by that time he probably will be brain dead. Now, last of all, I must ask if you want to donate his organs. He is young and has healthy organs that could be used to help save another life.

I was furious. I'm glad I didn't tell the doctor what I was thinking. "This is not a dog or some other kind of wild animal. This is my son, my flesh, and the one that most resembled me." He's only eighteen years old. This can't be happening to us. Someone must have made a mistake. These are things you read about in the paper and see on television, but this isn't supposed to happen to me. Two days earlier I was making plans to take my son hunting. I was helping him make the right decisions for his future. Now I'm being asked to make a decision about distributing his organs. My wife and I could not accept or deal with the fact that our son was shot and dying, so the very thought of him being torn apart and his organs distributed was more than we could bear. Please try to understand I am not trying to belittle the hospital, the doctor, or the professional services they rendered to us on this crucial day. Everyone seemed to be the bad guy that day, even God, and nobody knows his job better than Him.

I had to agree with my wife when she told the doctor we wanted them to do everything they possibly could for him. If the operation would do a little good, then little is better than none. If he came out as a vegetable, then a vegetable is better than a corpse. As far as the decisions, we would deal with them as they came.

The operation took several hours. In the meantime I called everyone I knew who could get a prayer through to God, to join with me in faith for a miracle. All over America, overseas, and in Canada there were people praying for us. I began to quote promises from the Bible. I have been called a "walking Bible" because of my ability to memorize whole chapters out of the bible. I made positive confessions. I couldn't accept what was happening. When we were finally allowed to see our son after the operation, they had moved him to the intensive care unit. His head was wrapped with surgical cloth and there seemed to be a dozen tubes and wires attached to his body. As I looked at him, I saw myself lying there. Everything about him reminded me of myself. A thousand memories flashed through my mind. I remembered our last conversation on that past Friday evening. You see I had not established the relationship that I wanted with my sons. When they were younger we did a lot of things together along with other kids at the church. As they grew older I wasn't there for them as much. I was busy trying to win souls for God, not knowing I was losing the one He had given me. In Jerome's preschool years he was sheltered from worldliness and quite active in the church. His teenage years brought on a spirit of rebellion. He ran away from home on many occasions. Each time he'd leave he'd cause a lot of conflict in our home between my wife and I. I finally told him, "You have an ultimatum. You can stay here as long as you like. If you leave, let us know where you are going and when you might be back. If you leave again without telling us, then I will decide when and if you can come back." I wasn't about to let an eighteen-year-old kid come in and out of our house and not abide by the rules that govern our household. I felt like I was losing my ability to be the man of the house. I was taught well if a man cannot rule his own house, he cannot rule the house of God. Well, my son did run away again. He was staying at this time with his older brother, who was sharing an apartment with his girlfriend. In our last conversation

I had agreed to let him come home and spend the weekend with us. Since Monday was a holiday, we made plans to get up early Tuesday morning and go job hunting. As our conversation came to a close, he spoke words to me that will be engraved in the memory bank of my mind until the day I die. Words that lift my spirit and fill my heart with joy each time I think about them, even to this day. I had never heard these words come from his lips. He said, "I love you, Dad." After a brief pause, I said, "I love you too, son." Then I hung up the phone. I was totally mesmerized by those powerful astonishing words. I know it's sad and even a bit shameful for me to admit it, but when I was growing up we didn't have the type of relationships in our family where we would say, I love you. I always thought that was mushy stuff men and women say to each other when they fall in love. I never really knew the power of those words. Even now they are some of the most powerful, meaningful words in my vocabulary, especially since they are the very last words I heard my son speak. Today, I teach men around the world to practice those words from their hearts and communicate the importance of them to their children before it is too late to be said. It's amazing how a man, like myself, who was approaching forty years old, had just learned about the foundation of what he had been preaching for years, 'love.'

By now the hospital waiting room and corridors were filled with family and friends. They would only allow two people at a time in to see Jerome, so each one was asked to make their visit brief. I walked the corridors praying and crying, frequently checking with the nurses to see if there were any changes. His condition would either stay the same or get worse. There was no improvement. When it was time for my wife and I to go back in to see Jerome, I had to face the painful reality he was dying. I prayed, I cried, I begged, I believed, and I pleaded, but yet still, he was dying. It was now time for me to stop thinking about myself and think about him. What about his salvation? Is he ready to meet God? I suddenly had to reassume my role as Pastor and not just father. I knew he had lived a life of sin and rebellion, but I remembered the promise God gave me years before, that my children would be saved. So I began to minister to him. I encouraged him to call on Jesus and accept Him as Lord and savior of his life. I had no way of knowing what his response would be. The doctor said he was in his final stages, but he could still hear us. I asked God for a sign that Jerome had made peace with him. As we prayed, one little tear rolled down his cheek. That tear was worth all the tears I had shed. I looked up at my wife and said, "Honey, we haven't failed. He's ready to go with Jesus. We did our best and God has honored that." My wife looked at me and said, "He really does love you. If I never believed that before, I believe it now."

It hadn't been but a few seconds after I left the room when they came and got me and said those most dreaded words, "He's gone." I turned around and saw my grief stricken wife running down the corridor screaming as she collapsed to the floor. I ran to assist her. After the nurses and I had calmed my wife, I locked arms with my other two sons, Micah and Edward. The three of us were weeping like helpless babies. I said to them, "You're all I have left now. Jerome is gone, he's gone, he's gone."

Jerome died about 2:00 a.m. It was by far the longest, most dreary night of my life. When we got home into bed, we couldn't sleep. After lying in bed a couple of hours, I got up and grabbed an old family album. I took all the pictures of Jerome out, from his baby pictures to the most recent ones. I spread them all over the dining room table and began weeping over them. It went from silent tears to mourns, then to a loud boisterous cry that woke the whole household (if any were really asleep) and the united cry started again.

When I finally did get to sleep it only lasted a couple of hours. I woke up hoping it was all just a really bad dream. But one look into the still teary eyes of my wife, who hadn't slept at all, and I knew I wasn't dreaming. Jerome had died. He left home never to return again. Nowhere on this earth could I go to find him. I had never been afraid to face my problems or

Apostle Eugene Satterwhite Th.D.

obstacles in the past. I did what many grieving people do, I turned my back on reality and tried to bury the truth in whatever felt good.

Erase It, Trace It, Or Face It

I recall a sermon I preached entitled, "Erase It, Trace It, or Face It." The message was like bitter medicine I was giving to an unwilling child and now was forced to take it myself. The good thing about it is that the medicine works. I would like to share with you some excerpts from this message that has helped so many:

Erase It

When you are faced with a problem or have to deal with difficulties, you can do one of three things, "Erase it, trace it, or face it." To erase it means you block it out of your mind or pretend it's not there. You never want to feel the pain or frustration so you just don't deal with it. How many times have you heard people say, "Don't talk to me about that, or I don't want to hear it, or I can't deal with that now?" Well, many times they are trying to erase problems they hope will just go away, but they won't. It's like a weed in the flower garden. You may go out and cut it off on the surface, but because it still has roots, it's coming up again. Many people only deal with surface things. They never go for the roots. Their actions are motivated by something more than what meets the eye.

Women who have been sexually assaulted may have a hard time adjusting in a relationship with the one they truly love. Their mate may think there's something wrong with him or he may feel threatened by his instability to satisfy her. There's a root cause to this problem that one must face in order to resolve it. The same principle goes for any given situation. Some people can talk about a murder without much reaction. But if you talk about a child molester or rapist, that same person will often get belligerent or vengeful. Chances are somewhere in their past they had to deal with rape or molestation. I react differently to hearing of a murder since I've lost a loved one to murder. I still have to face all of the issues and deal with my feelings of hate, bitterness, anger, and grief.

Trace It

People who trace their problem are the ones who dwell continually on them, but never do anything positive to change things. They are the ones who sit day in and day out watching the weeds in the flower garden and thinking about how beautiful the garden would be without them. They are the ones who generally end up in a mental institution. They are the ones with constant headaches, ulcers, high blood pressure, and diabetes from poor eating habits. They are the ones who die before their time because of sickness they brought on through worrying. You could never imagine how many times I relived that horrid scene at the hospital the night of Jerome's death. Over and over and over again, I'd think about what happened and ask, "why" I had to move on and face my trauma. It wasn't easy to accept. It wasn't easy to let go, but it was quite necessary. I was so used to trying to be everything for everybody. I would always try to be there to help others bear their pain and hardship. I was a shoulder to cry on, an ear to listen, and a friend to the one others had forsaken. Now I needed a shoulder, an ear to listen, and a friend that could go beyond human capability. I felt like there was only one set of footprints in the sand during those trying times.

Face It

To face it means to deal with reality. To look at your situation and deal with it in the most practical way possible. This means to see the weed in the flower garden, go over to it, take the necessary tools, dig it up from the roots, and then destroy it once and for all. Communication, counseling, support groups and therapy can all be tools for digging up roots. You must be willing to open up and talk about it. Although many times when we are faced with crises we don't always feel like talking about it. That's o.k. too, but remember the healing process generally won't begin until you are ready to release. Much of the grief that I would have held inside was released when I began to communicate my feelings to someone who was willing to listen. Communication gave me relief from pain that nothing else could give. If you are ministering to a grieving person, you should encourage them to talk without pressing them and assure them they can feel free to call you at any time. You must avail yourself to listen. It may be 3:30 a.m. when grief becomes so unbearable they must talk to someone. You must be willing to listen. Not judge or condemn and in some cases not even give your opinion, but just listen. You must allow yourself and others space to be human. Many people, especially leaders try to be the beacon light of hope for everyone else. They tell themselves, "I have to be strong for the sake of my children or those who are looking to me for strength." A person is really no strength to anyone if he's no strength to himself. Therefore, he must first be strong for himself. We must not be overtaken by guilt because we break down and weep or overreact in some situations. There is a grief process one will have to experience when they face tragedy or suffer loss. That process includes, but is not limited to, blaming God, others, and yourself. We may experience feelings of anger, resentment, isolation, and degradation. When these feelings occur we must remember we are fallible human beings and the pain and suffering can serve as a tool to get rid of these negative traits for good. Those who are ministering to hurting hearts must be sensitive enough to allow them space to be wrong. Don't misunderstand me. I'm not saying for you to compromise your faith, or let them live in error. Many times when a person is pouring out his heart, if you cut him off and start rebuking or correcting him, he will often freeze up and not talk to anyone again about the problem. This person may start to feel like no one understands or really cares what they are feeling. Let them get it all out first. There will be

Apostle Eugene Satterwhite Th.D.

time later for you to correct. Remember, we must first clean out the wound of infection before the healing process can begin.

A Part of Me

Thousands of thoughts engulf my mind
Memories magnetize the heart
Unanswered questions trouble the soul
As a puzzle missing a part

A vacant seat at our table
An empty spot on our pew
A voice missing from our choir
No earthy house to view

He left us in such sorrow
I've never felt such pain
A part of me is missing now
A part I can't regain

But God is still my refuge
He knows for me what's best
He said he'd never leave me
For that I can't regress

I must keep looking forward
Though paths seem long and dim
Love can't bring him back to me
But it can take me to him

Apostle Eugene Satterwhite Th.D.

Just When I thought Things Couldn't Get Worse

At a time in my life when I felt like I had hit rock bottom, I discovered there was still another awful bottom. I felt like I was floating on thin air reaching for the bottom which now seemed to be above my head. God, with His infinite mercy, had prepared me for this satirical year. For years, prior to 1989, I would go on a special fast and shut myself in at the church. I would offer to God the first fruit of my year. At midnight on New Year's Eve I would go immediately into my office into seclusion for several days. I would not see or talk to anyone but God during this time. The first time I went into seclusion, in 1980, I had never experienced such power. It was totally awesome. God's presence was so strong in the room I could hardly stand it. Then, on about the second day of the fast, God inspired me to pick up my pen and write as he gave me prophecies of major events that were forthcoming. Everything he spoke to me came to pass just as I had written. Since that time, every year when I go into my annual seclusion fast, God's spirit moves on me to write down major prophecies that are to take place that year. The prophecies for the year 1989 came differently than any other previous year. That year God gave me a word pertaining to my personal life and some of the hardships I would have to endure. I took it very lightly. I felt by the time I ended the 31 days of fasting and prayer, there would be nothing that could move me. How wrong I was. These are some of the things I wrote as God spoke to my heart:

"My son, prepare yourself. You will go through some things this year that will knock you off your feet and bring you to your knees. There will be a death in the Satterwhite family. Close friends will turn against you. Even fellow ministers will come against you to seek the destruction of your ministry. Satan will seek desperately to destroy your ministry. There will be a

vicious lie told about you that will shake your whole world, and your ministry will stand in jeopardy, but your faithfulness to me shall vindicate you. Be prepared to suffer much loss, but I will restore all things and you shall be blessed through it all."

    I stayed in seclusion for seven days that year. On the seventh night I came out and began a series of nightly revival meetings. I shared the prophecy with our congregation on the first night. I requested prayer for my family for strength to face what we were about to endure. When the Lord told me there would be a death in our family, I thought it would be a distant and much older relative. I never even imagined it would be my son. God saw me through one of the worst tests I believe a man could face. I didn't think things could get any worse, but they did. God had laid it upon my heart to stay at home for the first six months of the year and work with our local church. Normally, because of the Apostolic calling on my life, I would have been gone out assisting in the pioneering and establishing of churches, mainly on Indian reservations. God wanted me to be at home. My wife and I often think about how painful it would have been for her, had I not been there when Jerome got shot. It really does pay to know and obey God's voice.

    Since I was going to be home for six months I wanted to stay as busy as possible. Our church only had a few members, so I got involved in outreach ministries outside the church. I had been involved in prison ministry for about fifteen years. Purdy Correctional Institution for Women, was one of the places I'd go to minister. Our church would go on every fourth Sunday and hold a service for the women. We always drew a nice crowd and were well received. I decided to expand our ministry there. I spoke to the chaplain and she informed me that many of the women needed to be ministered to. The Chaplain's job was mainly administration and there was little time for her to pastor or be a shepherd to these women, of whom many were new converts. She got approval from her superiors to bring me in as a fill-in twice a week on her days off. I was classified as volunteer staff. When I came to the first gate of the institution I was given keys to all the offices in the building where the chapel was located. I was quite nervous about being in a place with so many lonely, hurting, and vulnerable women. I didn't want to ever be in any place alone at any time with any of these women. I made that known from the beginning.

My job was to check the chaplain's box on the days I was there (Monday and Tuesday) to see if anyone had turned in a request sheet to see the chaplain. If so, I would go to their ward and meet with them or set a time for counsel. I was given a portion of the guard's office for counseling. I felt safe because the office was fifty percent glass. Our system worked fine at first, then we started getting complaints about interruptions from the guards. We hardly get time in for prayer without a guard, another employee, or even an inmate just walking in. To resolve the problem, we decided to use the front part of the chapel office for prayer and counseling. I felt pretty safe there too because this was one of the most heavily populated areas in the institution at the time. Next to this office were other offices, the library, and an institutional school. There was a constant flow of traffic in the building. There was also a large picture window in the office that gave a view of the other wards and an open sports court. I thought it would be virtually impossible for me to be found in a compromising position. I had no idea of the pain and degradation I was about to face.

I'd stay busy at the institution from about 9:00 a.m. to 5:00 p.m. I'd have lunch and dinner there before I left. Most of my days were spent counseling and leading women to Christ. My days at Purdy were the most stressful days of my week. I would come home totally drained. I had done chaplain work in men's prisons for many years, but this was much more intense. I heard some of the most heartbreaking stories of how many of these women had been raped, abused and set up by their boyfriends, husbands, fathers, and other relatives. It was so easy for me to relate to their pain since I was still experiencing so much of it myself. I realize now I had only set myself up. I should have taken more time for my own healing. I was giving out the love and comfort I really needed for myself. I've learned if you are seeking counsel from someone and they tell you they are in the same situation you are in, you had better run for your life. They cannot pull you out of a ditch they themselves have fallen into. I learned as a leader when you give out so much, you have to keep enough for yourself or you won't be any help to anyone else. The hardest thing for a person who is a giver to do, is to receive.

Things went well for about three or four months at Purdy. Then, I remember that cold, cloudy day when I arrived at the institution and was approached by two security guards. They told me I couldn't go in until I talked to the superintendent who had been awaiting my arrival. It was Saturday, the 19th of June. This was one of the biggest days of the year for the black inmates. It was their Juneteenth celebration. It was considered the black Americans Fourth of July, celebrating their freedom from slavery. I had been rehearsing some songs and poetry with the inmates in preparation for this day. When the superintendent came out to the gate where I was waiting, he told me I had been temporarily banned from the institution because there had been allegations of sexual misconduct. He said, "I can't give you any more information on it but a detective will be contacting you shortly." I was floored by his caustic words. My heart felt like a bomb ready to explode at any moment. "There's got to be some kind of mistake," I said. I've worked in prison ministry all these years, and never had an incident or even the slightest complaint. My record was perfect. I'd always given my best in everything I had done. Why would someone do this to me? Though I left the institution in tears, I had a sense of relief knowing I was innocent. I had a rough road ahead of me. Now, I must go home and face my still grieving wife and tell her I had been accused of sexual misconduct. I didn't know who, what, when, how, or where. I remembered on my last day at Purdy I led three women to Christ. My conduct there had always been on a professional level.

My wife is a loving, trusting person. She stood with me through the whole ordeal, even after we found it was not only

Apostle Eugene Satterwhite Th.D.

sexual misconduct that I was being accused of, but rape. That evening I was scheduled to go out of town for one of my away from home revival meetings in Missouri. I again set out to go minister with a hurting heart. As I look back on my life, I wonder how I was able to go on without having a nervous breakdown.

When I arrived home from Missouri, I didn't wait for a detective to contact me. I contacted him. I was anxious to find out who was saying such horrible things about me. When I finally was allowed to read the charges, I was totally heartbroken. It was a seventeen year old inmate who had met with me in the chaplain's office to share with me some of her poetry. I'm a great lover of poetry and often share poetry along with my sermons. She seemed so nice and innocent. I would never have expected anything like this from her. Later, I learned that she and some of the other inmates had discussed a case where a female inmate had been raped by a staff member. The inmate not only was granted release, but was also awarded one million dollars in damages. This gave my accuser incentive to go after me. Her claim was that while we were in our counseling session, I was relating to the death of my son and broke down in tears. Because she was also going through some trauma in her life, she began crying. In our efforts to console each other, she claims I became this vicious animal who went into a sexual rage rubbing my hands all over her body. Then I allegedly twisted her arm and forced her into the adjoining locked room with one hand, and with the other hand I removed her pants and raped her. Though I was outraged by the accusations, there was calmness in my heart. I knew once an investigation was done the truth would come forth and I could go on with my life.

Several weeks passed and I heard no word from the detective or the prosecutor. I just knew they had come to the realization the inmate was lying and I was the victim in this case. It didn't happen that way. It was in the heat of August when I had just ended a powerful revival in Spokane, Washington. Many souls were saved and added to the church. On that Wednesday, there was a prophetess who called all the ministers to the side to request prayer for me. She said God revealed to her I was about to undergo a vicious satanic attack. That was an understatement to me when I discovered what was ahead. The revival ended Friday, and on Saturday morning the news came. My mother called from Tacoma. She was crying. She said, "It's on the front page of the local newspaper. The lies the inmate told about you have been published in the news." She then read the article to me. I felt like my whole world had just come to an end. Things the media wrote about Jimmy Swaggard and Jim Baker were nice compared to what they had written about me. The reason the story was published was because the prosecutor decided to go ahead and file charges against me. The newspaper picked up the report from the court documents and printed only what the girl had said. I was now on the menu of nearly every newspaper, television, and radio broadcast throughout the state of Washington. When I hung up the phone, I ran upstairs to the room where I was staying, threw myself on the bed and wept. The local pastor tried to comfort me to no avail. This is it, I thought, my life is over. Everything I've ever done for God was in vain. Fifteen years of volunteer prison work and this was my reward? Then, in a still small voice, the Lord spoke to my heart and reminded me of what he had said at the beginning of the year. *"There will be a vicious lie told about you that will shake your whole world and your ministry will stand in jeopardy, but your faithfulness to me shall vindicate you."* The Lord further instructed me to pray for my accuser because judgment would follow her and her family until she came forth with the truth. Sure enough, within days of God's speaking this to me, tragedy hit her life and there was death and judgment even though I had prayed for her. It is really hard to pray for someone who's trying to destroy you when all you did was try to lead them to salvation.

Now I was in for another real test of my faith. I had to prepare for trial. First, I needed an attorney. I learned so much about our judicial system I had never known. I learned it has everything to do with money. One well known attorney told me he didn't care if I had done it or not. "Give me twelve thousand dollars and I'll get you off." I walked out of his office in a hurry. I needed someone who believed I was innocent. It was hard for me to find an attorney I could afford. The Lord blessed me to find an attorney who would work with me on a payment plan for his services.

I must conclude the trial was something God ordained for me to endure because everything about the case was out of the norm. The prosecutor, who was a very biased female, had absolutely no evidence at all, yet she filed charges on the word of a convicted felon alone. It is quite ironic how a person who is incarcerated for attempted murder and burglary and has a history of prostitution, can make an accusation and get it published in the news media around the state. Yet, a pastor, who has served the community for nearly twenty years and never had a record, was never contacted or given an opportunity to defend himself before his name was scandalized. The prosecutor's case was so weak the first thing she did when we arrived in court was to drop the charges from second degree rape to third degree. An examination of the inmate's body showed not even a trace of sexual activity. Her clothes were examined also, but there was nothing. The prosecutor went through the institution trying to find evidence and could find none. Not one woman could testify that my behavior, while there, was unprofessional. The prosecutor was even given a letter in which my accuser confessed to lying. The inmate said she hated men and she finally found one she could make pay. Because of the victim shield law, the judge would not allow the jury to see the letter, because it revealed her lesbian activity and her past history as a prostitute. I learned there are laws that could let an innocent man go to jail in order to protect a so called victim. The judge that handled our case was a rookie. It was his very first case. You would think rookies would start out in traffic violations or something less severe.

When I realized we were going all the way with this trial, I prayed and asked God for justice I knew I couldn't get from man. I asked God to bless me with jury members that were Christians. God answered my prayer. Everything I asked for seemed to be granted. I seemed to have special favor with God during these trying times. One day during the trial, my attorney called a special meeting with the judge, the prosecutor, and myself. "Something has come up," he said. "My assistant (a born-again believer) was out last night playing basketball. His church was playing against another church. At the end of the game, they joined hands to have a closing prayer. One of the players from the other team made a prayer request to the group. He said, "I was selected for jury duty. It is a case concerning a minister who is being charged with rape." The judge and prosecutor all agreed no damage was done and this incident would not affect the case. I just began to rejoice because God had answered my prayers. Out of over two hundred thousand people in Tacoma and the surrounding areas, God brought together the right people at the right time to let me know he had heard and answered my prayers. What an awesome God!

What happened to me during this trial was like something right out of the pages of the Bible. I saw God at work on my behalf the way I'd never seen before. The pastor from Spokane was with me during the trial. One morning before we went to court he told me the Lord had given him a scripture for me, which was *Psalms 27:1-5*. One of the verses in this passage of the scripture says: *"When the wicked even mine enemies and my foes, came upon me to eat up my flesh, they stumbled and fell."* It was a coincidence, but when we got to court, the prosecutor came in, tripped, and dropped all her papers on the floor.

On our first day of the trial, it was snowing quite heavily. The judge made an announcement if it continued to snow, he would postpone the trial for another time. He advised everyone to stay at home if there was lots of snow on the ground the next day. That night, I rose in the middle of the night to see snowflakes violently falling from the sky. Tears filled my eyes as I began to think about the case being postponed. "Lord," I prayed, "I've been through enough pain and humiliation." My youngest son was still in high school and he had to live with the reproach also. "I'm tired, and I just want it all to be over." Then all of a sudden my pity party turned to faith. I felt like the spirit of Elijah had come upon me as I raised my hand toward heaven and said, "If I be a man of God, let this snow cease now." I sat and watched in awesome wonder and amazement as the snow drizzled down to a complete halt. I couldn't believe my eyes. Then like Gideon, I decided to put it to the test. I knew when I told this story people would not believe God had stopped the snow just for me. So, I asked God for a sign, to hold back the snow until after the jury reached its verdict. Then, once the case was over, let it snow in record-breaking inches. This way I would be sure God did this for me and me alone. This prayer was made on a Wednesday. It did not snow again until Friday. On Friday, the judge made a statement and said, "This case will not be finished today and Monday is a holiday so the case will probably be postponed until another date." I then began to pray. I said, "Lord, you showed me you answered my prayer by placing some Christians on the jury, so Lord speak to their hearts and let them return the not guilty verdict within one hour."

Praise God; within thirty-five minutes the verdict was in. I never will forget that magical moment when the judge came out of his chamber and announced the jury had reached its verdict. The clerk then turned and said, "look at all the snow coming down. It's really sticking. It's been awhile since we had snow like this." Tears welled up in my eyes. Nobody can convince me, to this day, God didn't do it just for me. The jury came forth with a "not guilty" verdict and the newspaper cleared my name as much as they could. In the eyes of some people, if you are a preacher, you're guilty. I must reluctantly say my biggest persecution came from so-called Christians. People on the street would encourage me. They knew the games inmates played. But the so called Christians would make little cunning remarks that would pierce my soul. I thank God for giving me strength to go through. I see now God has honored me with experience that can be beneficial in his kingdom. I said I wanted to be used by

God. God has put me on his display shelf. Whenever someone comes to God crying because they have suffered a loss or have been falsely accused, God says to them, *"I have just the person for you."* Then he reaches up on his display shelf and gets me.

Apostle Eugene Satterwhite Th.D.

If God Were Like Man

I am very Thankful, to be under God's command.
How insecure my hope would be, if God were like man.

Man would probably give me up, before I got a start.
While he looks on my outward parts, God looks at my heart.

Man is so unmerciful; God's mercy is everlasting.
With man I can beg and beg and beg, With God it's mine for the asking.

Then if man had the power, to wash away my sin.
Then every time when vexed with me, He'd bring them up again.

And every time I faltered, He would not understand.
How insecure my hope would be, if God were like man.

And when I have hard trials, although I've done my best.
In man I'd find no comfort, I'd find no place of rest.

Then if I got in trouble, He'd only hold a grudge.
He would not be my lawyer; He'd only be my judge.

He'd judge me when I prospered, He'd judge me when I fail.
And if just once, I lost connection, my soul would be bound for hell.

Man is so impatient, that I'd have no second chance,
How insecure my hope would be, if God were like man.

But God is the one that made me; He'll always lead my life.
In Him there's no confusion, In Him there is no strife.

He knows when I mean business, He knows if I'm a fake.
He knows when I falter on purpose, Or whether by mistake.
He doesn't make false promises; He lives up to his name.
Though man changes day by day, My God He's still the same.

I could not lean on the arm of flesh; it would be like sinking sand.
How insecure my hope would be, if God were like man.

Apostle Eugene Satterwhite Th.D.

Why Me, Lord?

A well-known quote says, "What you don't know won't hurt you." Since our decisions should be based on our knowledge, then what we don't know can be very detrimental to us. Life's issues should be dealt with from a knowledgeable point of view. The facts should be known before judging or deciding on any given thing. People often say, "Don't question God. He does what he pleases, and even if it shatters your life and crushes all your dreams, just accept it as God's will and not question him." Well, this is also error. Most of the great men of the Bible questioned God when things didn't go as they should. As a father, I would not punish or allow negative things to happen to my children and not be willing to tell them why. As a child, if my father walked into the room and started spanking me in front of all my friends, my first question would be, Why? Why are you hurting and embarrassing me? If I can ask my earthly father why, then I can also ask my heavenly father. Even going through the normal tests and trials of a Christian believer is much easier to endure when you know why. Every trial you face can, in one way or another, fall into one of these four categories:

1) The trying of your faith – *James 1:3 and 1 Peter 1:12*
2) The results of a bad decision – *Deuteronomy 11:26-28*
3) Reaping what you sow – *Galatians 6:7*
4) Your season – *Ecclesiastes 3:1, Psalms 1:3, and Galatians 6:9*

The Trying Of Your Faith

Knowing this that the trying of your faith worketh patience. James 1:3 Beloved, think not it strange concerning the fiery trial which is to try you, as though some strange thing happened unto you. 1 Peter 4:12

Some things we go through in this life are no more than a test of our faith. Things happen to us many times to let us know where we are. The Bible teaches us we are purified by fire as a gold and silver refiner purifies his gold and silver. Fire burns out all the impurities. Our fiery trials as mentioned in *1 Peter 4:12*, are designed to bring us closer to God. They will either bring us closer to God or drive us farther from him. I believe something spiritual is taking place during those trying times. You are being made. *James 1:3* says, *"Knowing this, that the trying of your faith worketh patience."* God wants us to know our suffering is not in vain. He wants us to know our trials can work for us. I have a slogan that says, "When trials come to visit you, put them to work." It is time to put our problems and hardships to work and stop letting them work us. They can be an employer or an employee. If you make your trials work for you, you can call the shots. You are the boss. You can allow them to build characteristics of Christ in your life. They can bring you patience and longsuffering. They can teach you faith and courage. If you make them your employer they will bring you anger, bitterness, hatred, jealousy, and ungratefulness. You can lose control.

There was a man who went into a potter's house. The potter had a great display of beautiful vessels that were finished, and some were still in the making. As the man beheld all the vessels in the oven being tempered for final display, he asked the potter, "How do you know when a vessel is ready to come out of the oven or the fire?" The potter slowly walked over to the oven where a vessel had been baking for some time and was ready to come out. He took the vessel and thumped it on the side with his fingers. From the vessel came forth a tune. "When it starts to sing," said the potter, "It's ready to come out." God will often allow us to go through hardships until we have a change of attitude that will cause us to sing and praise God in all things. In *Acts 16:25*, Paul and Silas prayed and sang praise to God in the midst of their persecution. They had been falsely accused and beaten, yet they still had a song. No matter what we lose in this life, all is not lost if we still have a song.

The lesson is learned by our going through. God could just move the problem and rid us of the pain, but what would we learn? It is like the children of Israel at the Red Sea. God could have just moved the whole sea out of their way, but instead he made a way for them to go through it. In so doing, he created a means by which he could destroy their enemy so they could never be taken in bondage again. It's amazing how God takes our hardships and uses them to defeat our enemies. Including things like pride, lust, impatience, etc. *1 Corinthians 10:13* says, *"God is faithful, who will not suffer you to be tempted above that ye are able; but will with the temptation make a way to escape."* In this scripture we find a package deal. It lets us know trials come not alone, but with a way out. We must stop focusing on the trial or temptation and start seeking God for his way of escape.

The Results Of A Bad Decision

Behold, I set before you this day a blessing and a curse; a blessing, if ye obey the commandments of the Lord your God, which I command you this day; and a curse, if ye will not obey the commandments of the Lord your God, but turn aside out of the way, which I command you this day, to go after other gods, which ye have not known. Deuteronomy 11:26-28

If I went outside in freezing weather, with no shoes and no shirt and caught an awful cold, I couldn't say it is the trying of my faith. If I continue to drive my car when the gas gauge is empty, and I run out of gas, I can't say it is the trying of my faith. No, it is the result of a bad decision. We are faced with important decisions every day. These decisions can determine the outcome of the rest of our lives. One thing God gave us is the freedom of choice. God does not force us to do the right thing. He gives us his written word, the bible, as a guideline for making our decisions in life. Most people choose not to follow the instructions in the Bible. When they start to experience the painful results of their bad decision they often get angry and start pointing the finger at God. They blame God for something they never let him have a part in to begin with. When we do things on our own, we are on our own. The Bible says in *Proverbs 3:6, "In all thy ways acknowledge him, and he shall direct thy paths."* God has a plan of success for all our lives. If we would seek him for direction he would lead us to the paths that are most beneficial to us. Most people only pray once a day or should I say, once a night before they crawl into bed. I believe God would rather we pray in the morning by giving him the first fruit of our day. We should not wait until we've already blown it before seeking his direction. I often tell the people I counsel "Don't come to me for advice if you've already decided what you're going to do." Many people are crying out to God for direction, but they have no intention of following Him when He does speak. Nothing is more frustrating to me than when a person seeks counsel after the fact. They didn't consider counsel when they decided to get married. Your advice meant nothing. When their marriage is going poorly, then they want to seek help and counsel. The only way to avoid making bad decisions is to acknowledge God first and let him direct us. I am reminded of a song God gave me at the beginning of the year:

"I Need To Hear A Word From You"

I need to hear a word from you,
So I'll know what to do.
I never had to make decisions on my own,
I need to hear your voice,
Before I make my choice.
In every endeavor,
I need you more than ever,
I know I cannot make it alone,
Lord, I need to hear a word from you.

Apostle Eugene Satterwhite Th.D.

Reaping What You Sow

Be not deceived, God is not mocked, for whatsoever a Man soweth, that shall he also reap. Galatians 6:7

Life is governed by laws of sowing and reaping: "What goes up, must come down." No one can change this. Everyone will reap what they sow. In *Galatians 6:7*, the apostle Paul spoke to the church of Galatia and compared their conduct to a farmer sowing seeds in his field. He said, *"Be not deceived, God is not mocked,"* whatever you plant is what you will harvest. We must realize that our actions today will affect us when we are older. For instance, I may love to eat a lot of fatty, unhealthy food when I'm twenty. If I continue with my bad eating habits, at forty, I will have an overweight, unhealthy body that will probably be accompanied by diabetes, high blood pressure, and heart problems. I often wondered how drug addicts and alcoholics could continue abusing their bodies when they see what the drugs and alcohol has done to their friends. They watched their friends die but that is no deterrent for them. Then, there are those who are homosexual or sexually perverted, who watch their friends die of AIDS, but that is still not enough to make these people change their lifestyles. The Lord let me see how many Christians are the same way when it comes to eating. I, for one, have watched faithful men and women die before their time because of some disease brought on by overeating and eating too much of the wrong things. Many of these people went to their graves thinking their sickness was a trying of their faith, when it was no more than reaping what they had sowed earlier in life. Another well-known quote is "a wise man learns from his mistakes." But I say, "a wiser man will learn from the mistakes of others." A wise man need not become an addict to learn about drugs. He can see the devastating effects drugs have on friends, loved ones, and the whole community. There's nothing in this life you can go through that someone hasn't already been through. That's one of the reasons we have the Bible. So that we can learn from the mistakes of the patriarchs and not make the same mistakes. Our actions and our words are seeds that will spring up one day and either produce for us a fruitful or a corrupt harvest. As I look back over my life I wish I had done things differently. Many people deceive themselves by saying, "If I could turn back the hands of time and do it all over, I'd do things differently." I do not feel this is truthful. If we are not willing to change today as a result of the mistakes of yesterday, then if we relived yesterday we wouldn't change. Everyday is a gift from God for us to improve on yesterday's failure, for tomorrow's success.

Your Season

To everything there is a season, and a time to every purpose under the heaven. Ecclesiastes 3:1

And he shall be like a tree planted by the rivers of water that bringeth forth his fruit in his season; his leaf also shall not wither; and whatsoever he doeth shall prosper. Psalms 1:3

And let us not be weary in well doing: for in due season we shall reap, if we faint not. Galatians 6:9

These scriptures give us to know there is a season for all things. A man's life is like the four seasons of the year. There are rainy days and sunny days. There are storms and hurricanes. There are tornadoes and earthquakes. I wish we could all live in spiritual greenhouses where the temperature never changes, and we were watered and fed only as needed, and we never had to experience the storm. We would then probably never pray or trust in God's strength to sustain us. There are four undisputable facts about storms:

1) Everyone is affected – A storm may come to your area and not have as great an impact on you as others, but by the time the Governor declares a state of emergency, tax dollars will be called for that will affect all. Likewise

when a Christian goes through a storm the impact should affect other Christians.
2) Storms don't come to stay – A person who hates snow doesn't go out and commit suicide when it snows, because he knows they will pass. So why turn your back on God when you face hardships? It will pass.
3) You can't stop hardships and storms from coming – *Man that is born of a woman is of few days, and full of trouble. Job 14:1*
4) You can't make them leave – *All the days of my appointed time, will I wait, till my change comes. Job 14:14*

Before you ask God, "Why me?" ask yourself, why not me? The prayerful seek God for his purpose in allowing them to go through. If God allows me to go through the fire, then there is something in the fire he wants me to gain. There's always something in the fire for me. Bible patriarchs such as Daniel, Joseph, Shadrach, Meshach, and Abednego, got their promotions after they came out of the fire. This reminds me of a message I recently preached entitled: "I'm Coming Out, But I'm Not coming Till I Get What I Went In For." When I was a child, my mother would send me to the store with a list. If I didn't get what I went for I had to go back. Get the picture? While you are in the fire, instead of trying to rush out, look to see what God has for there so you won't have to go back over and over. If there is patience for you in the fire, stay there until you get it. We must not view suffering as a terrible obstacle meant to take us down. Look at our suffering as an opportunity to show God's power in rising up above the storm.

He's Mindful

Sometimes in this journey it seems we are alone,
But God is mindful of us.
We wonder if in Him we've spiritually grown,
He's still mindful.

We work and we sweat, seems like down to our bones,
Yet it seemed like so little of good we have sown,
And will God accept such little we've shown.
Yes, 'cause he's mindful.

If we try to live here below free from sin,
He is mindful.
With a little encouragement now and then,
He's mindful.
We feel we are finished; we've only begun,
We feel things are bad; they'll get worse my friend.
There's a better day coming, God only knows when,
But he's mindful.

We serve a God that sees, knows, and cares,
And he's mindful.
He knows just how much of a load we can bear,
'Cause he's mindful.

We look in our cabinet, the cabinet is bare,
We open our wallet, there's no money there,
We open our closets, no fine clothes to wear,
It seems that no one will share their goods with us,
But he's mindful.

Apostle Eugene Satterwhite Th.D.

Now we do get discouraged and sometimes we feel,
He's not mindful.
But in that sad moment, he does not appear,
To be mindful.
We search and we search, to get a refill,
We strive every day to stay in his will.
Oh Satan will come to destroy and to kill,
But remember one thing that our God is real.
Really mindful.

When life's road is traveled, we've done all we can,
He's mindful.
He'll meet us in heaven with a welcoming hand,
Yes, he's mindful.
I'm looking forward to meeting the man,
Who's kept me safe from Satan's hand.
Who's helped me in perilous times to stand,
That Holy, than meek and that merciful man,
Who's been mindful.

The Physical, Mental, And Spiritual Aspects of Grief

Dr. Webster defines grief as: keen mental suffering or distress over affliction or loss; sharp sorrow, painful regret, bereavement, dolor, etc. The Greek word, "Lupe" signifies pain of body or mind. To thoroughly cover the subject of grief one must consider the physical, mental, and spiritual aspect of grief, since man is a triune being, made of body, soul, and spirit. The body is the physical, the soul is the mental, and the spirit is the spiritual.

The Physical Aspect

Our body is affected by the changes that take place in spirit and soul. The body is composed of flesh, blood, and bones. Although man is spirit, he possesses a soul and lives in a body. Someone once said, "The body is where we live, but the soul is who we are."

Grief seems to take its greatest toll on the body. The first thing grief seems to do is rob you of strength. Note when people get down in heart and spirit they are down in the body. Have you ever seen a person that was energetically discouraged or enthusiastically depressed? When a person is down it makes their physical body weak. You can be so down you have no strength to fight. You may be surrounded with spiritual warfare weapons, but are too weak to use them. Grief will drain you and open the door for discouragement. When discouragement comes in; the devil puts a prop in the door so any and every other spirit can enter in. Things we normally would not allow to hinder us are now a perfect excuse for not going to church, to work, or doing things we know are necessary to bring the happiness we desire. When our bodies are weak we become slothful and lazy. We know we have the ability to overcome some of the petty things that flair up in our lives but we are not in the physical shape to fight. Therefore, we accept defeat. If we continue to allow the soul realm to dictate the actions of our bodies, it will soon take its toll and end with physical illness. You may start worrying and develop ulcers. Bitterness sets in and blood pressure rises. Tension is at its maximum as the body starts to go down fast. We start treating the symptoms, but not the cause. We take pills that only cause us problems in other areas. We begin to fight a spiritual war using natural weapons.

If a person is experiencing grief that is accompanied by unforgiveness, the healing process will take much longer. Healing in this case, must start with the inner man. Doctors world wide have proven the largest percent of all sicknesses stems, in one way or another, from unforgiveness. The best way to get back at an enemy who has wronged you is to forgive him. In doing so you rob him of the ability to bring further harm to you. When you harbor unforgiveness, you give your enemy a tool to bring sickness and death.

After my son was shot I was reluctant to continue in the prison ministries I had been involved with for many years. I feared coming face to face with the man that brutally took my son's life. From my standpoint, justice had not been served. There was never a trial. The man was given a light sentence under a plea bargain agreement. There was no reason for the prosecutor to offer a plea bargain, it was a clear-cut case. The witness and the evidence were all intact. In addition, the accused man didn't deny killing my son. I had a lot of unforgiveness built up in my heart. I hated our justice system. I hated my son's killer. I hated the girls that lied about me and caused my name to be scandalized. The same system that denied the evidence and plea-bargained with a light sentence for my son's killer took the word of a convicted felon with absolutely no evidence at all and prosecuted a case against me. I had become quite popular at the state prisons, because of the ministry I'd rendered for years. I received letters from inmates offering to take care of the injustice I had received. That wasn't God's way.

"Vengeance is mine saith the Lord." Though it was tempting, I had to rebuke those thoughts of revenge out of my mind. For years I had preached about unforgiveness and hatred. I would have never believed, before this year that a pastor like myself, who stood so firmly against an eye for an eye, would find himself embracing them. I thank God today I am delivered. I can look anyone in the eyes and say from my heart, "I love you," after God brought deliverance to me. I could genuinely let them know that I had forgiven them. When my deliverance from unforgiveness and hatred came, I was not in a powerful revival or crusade; no one laid their hands on me to try to cast out these negative spirits. I simply read God's word and decided I was not going to live my life in the miserable state I was in. So, I decided to forgive. I choose to love. Knowing that to err is human, but to forgive is divine, I sought God's intervention. Through his power working in me, I was able to forgive the unforgettable, and love the unlovable.

Crying is another part of our grieving process that is necessary for healing. Crying is our bodies' way of expressing the emotions of the soul and spirit. Crying can be one of the most misinterpreted expressions man can give. Some people cry when they are happy, and others when they are sad. In this day and time, men have deemed tears a sign of weakness. I beg to differ. The cry of courage calls for faith and hope, but the cry of pity calls for pity. The cry of courage is healthy. When we cry our bodies release a chemical stored by stress that brings healing to our body. The words of the following poem sum it all up:

Apostle Eugene Satterwhite Th.D.

Tears

Thousands of tears are shed daily, for one reason or another
The cry of help for one in need, or an infant for his mother

Tears of sorrow, tears of joy, tears of hope and cheer
At a wedding ceremony, or the loss of someone dear

Some say it's a sign of weakness, I certainly disagree
God doesn't waste the tears shed unto Him, He turns them into victory

Tears have built many churches, they have cleared pathways blocked
Someone cried out to God in prayer, and impossible doors were unlocked

We remember Hezekiah, when told he was going to die
He turned his face unto the wall, and to his maker he began to cry

When God heard his faithful servant, he gathered up all those tears
There must have been fifteen bottles, he turned them into years

Then there was the prophet Jonah, who disobeyed God's voice
When he ended up in the belly of the whale, he knew he'd made the wrong choice

When God heard the cry of Jonah, it was time to move his hand
Those tears must have made the old whale sick, he spat Jonah up on dry land

Then there was blind Bartimaeus, who by the wayside cried
Jesus thou Son of David, I will not be denied

Though the multitude tried to stop him, he cried with all his might
When Jesus heard this blind man cry, he gave him back his sight

So let us cry out to God with travailing, from life's burdens we'll find relief
Never cry tears of self pity, they only leave stains of grief

Praying the intercessory prayer, brings light in our darkest hour
Tears and faith blended together is the recipe for power

Apostle Eugene Satterwhite Th.D.

The Mental Aspect

There was a case that came up in my studies in psychology, of a boy who was physically abused by his father. His father had a problem dealing with his anger. He would make the boy stand up against the wall, he would then proceed with beating the child for any reason or no reason at all. He took all of his frustrations out on his helpless son. After years of his abuse the boy found a way to escape the pain. As he stood there with his face to the wall being whipped, he would think or imagine himself going right through the wall. Once he was on the other side of the wall, the painful lashes from his father's belt could no longer be felt. To him, the father was hitting the wall. Though the painful lashes often drew blood, the son felt nothing.

In another case there was a group of college students who were used to show how powerful the mind is. The experimenters planned two parties where alcohol was supposed to be served in their beverage. They reacted the same at both parties, like drunken college students. The only problem was at the second party there was no alcohol at all in the punch. They were only told that alcohol was in the punch, and the punch was made to taste like there was alcohol in it. As the students drank the punch they thought they were getting drunk. They started acting like they were drunk. It was all in their minds.

To discover the mental aspects of grief, we must deal with the soul. The soul of man is incorporated with his will, mind, and emotions. The human brain is the most complex, most intricately designed mechanism known to man. Man has built computers that will store billions of pieces of information, but they can't surpass the human brain. I'm told if you were to take the cells from a single human brain and put them in a straight line there would be enough cells to take you to the moon and back. Although we only use a small portion of our brain, with that small portion we have built skyscrapers and gone to the moon.

When negative grief settles in the mind you will begin losing the battle. Your way of thinking changes. Your thoughts start running wild. You may start thinking and acting like everyone is against you, even God. You will soon become distant to friends and God. You see people smiling and laughing and will wonder why they are so happy. What are they smiling about? You start to think everyone should feel your pain. If you confide in someone you may get upset because they don't seem to feel what you feel. The hurt you feel from one person, you may cause to another. This is just the beginning of your spiritual demise. When you are grieved and depressed about one thing, grief has a way of reminding you about all the other negative things that are happening or have happened. It will send your mind wandering back years into your past to nurture on bad experiences you'd almost forgotten. The pity party of the mind is now in full swing. You drink the wine of oppression as you dance with despair. Then the main attraction is offered, "P.L.O.M." punch, poor, little, ole me. You start to block out all positive thoughts. Since our actions are motivated by our thinking he's dumb; he'll act like a nut case. If you think you're a loser, you've lost. As a man thinketh in his heart, so is he. Your mind is so powerful you can often think yourself into sickness or well-being. My mother ran an adult family home, where one of her clients was a hypochondriac, intense worrying would cause him to believe he had certain medical conditions in his body. His strong belief in the existence of these diseases in his body would often send him to the hospital to be treated for actual symptoms of a condition that never existed. If the mind has that much power in the negative realm, think of what positive thinking might do. The success in any battle in life, whether sports, academic achievement, physical well- being, or reaching economic goals, all starts in the mind. You must believe you can.

If one refuses to revert to positive thinking and continues a line of negativity, soon he will be faced with a spirit of hopelessness. When hopelessness sets in, then you just want to die. This is why there are so many suicides. People don't know how to deal with hopelessness, so they just end it all. Almost everyone that has lived any length of time has come to a point in their lives when they thought they wanted to die. Even great Bible patriarchs came to a point in their lives when they wanted to die. For example:

> *David said, "...Oh that I had wings like a dove! For Then would I fly away, and be at rest." Psalm 55:6*
>
> *Job said, "Oh that I might have my request; and that God would grant me the thing that I long for!"*
>
> *Even that it would please God to destroy me; that he would let loose his hand, and cut me off! Job 6:8-9*
>
> *Elijah said, "...It is enough; now Oh Lord, take away my life; for I am not better than my fathers." 1 Kings 19:4*

These men were all faced with trauma and grief, but if you read the rest of their stories you'll find they all went on to fulfill their great call and purpose in life. They did not allow their temporal emotions to get in the way of God's eternal will and plan for their lives. God has a plan for all our lives and if we gear our minds to look beyond what meets the eye, we will see purpose and meaning in our existence. Hope will again come alive. Hope will use its authority to stop the music in your mind and bring the pity party to an end. Hope will then invite his closest relatives Joy and Peace and they will serve happiness as the main entrée.

The Spiritual Aspect

Once negative influence has conquered the body and soul now he must corrupt the spirit. The spirit of man is the God part. Before a man comes to God for salvation, his spirit man is dead as stated in *Ephesians 2:12*. That means you did what you felt like doing and most of us had no conscience for our wrongdoing. Although our soul and spirit are separate, they are inseparable. They penetrate each other. The dividing of the soul and spirit come through God's word, as stated in *Hebrews 4:12*. The spirit of man instinctively yearns for God, while the soul yearns for the flesh, and the lust thereof. When you are too weak in your body to fight grief, and you have your mind programmed for defeat, your spirit will soon lose conscience; you will revert back to evil passions. You then take on a perverse spirit that will become as fuel for the body and soul to act out corrupt desires for a temporal fulfillment. Remember, temporal fulfillment can never be substituted for eternal desire. It's like an auto manufacturer who has the technology to build a trouble-free vehicle that would last for years. That would soon put him out of business, so he makes an automobile that will keep the buyer dependent on him. I once owned a car I had to take back to the dealer just to have the headlights changed. A special tool that most shops didn't have. That's the way God designed man. He created him from the dust of the earth. If he would have ended there, man would be no more than a dog, a cow, or anything else God made, but man is special to God. What makes man different is that God breathed in his nostrils the breath of life and man became a living soul. In other words, God used of himself as it were fuel to light the candle of human life, thus giving his creation eternal dependency on Him for his fulfillment. To be fulfilled means to be satisfied, or bring a longing to an end. It means to finish or complete. Fulfillment must start with the mind and end with the spirit of man being in complete fellowship with God. This is what constitutes the fulfillment of man. Whatever a thing is made of, is what it will take to make it function properly. The body came from the earth, therefore the things that come from the earth such as herbs, fruits, and vegetables are the things that are best for the body, and help us operate more fluently. Sixty percent of our body liquid consists of water. Therefore, our body is dependent on water for its existence. Our body rejects and reacts negatively to anything foreign that comes in.

The same concept works with the spirit of man. If you are a person who is spiritual and walking by God's word, your spirit will react and reject carnality. If you are carnal, the spirit man has been dethroned and the carnal nature is alive. It is saying, feed me. Because man lacks the knowledge or awareness of his desire for God's spirit, he tries to fulfill them in other ways. The brain of man has a central pleasure point. Once it reaches its euphoria, the memory of it is stored. There are neurotransmitters, (a living network of brain cells in continual communication) that cross the space between one brain cell and the next to enable communication between cells. The dopamine pathway connects the limbic system to the cortex. Dopamine also participates in the brains rewards system and in the control of motor activity. Dopamine works with other chemicals or drugs such as crack cocaine, to help one reach the euphoria. That's why many people get hooked on crack, sex, or alcohol after just one experience. This is why people who are backslidden from God seem to go to the extreme in sin. They are trying to fill a void only God can fill. When a man is saved and in fellowship with God, his maker, he reaches an ultimate euphoria in life. Nothing thereafter can take the place of God's presence in his life.

Interviews with the rich and famous have revealed that many of them, even though they have achieved great success and gained material wealth, will confess there is still a void in their lives. There is only one void I know of that can't be filled by fortune or fame, by power or position, and by friendship and family. That void is God's spirit in man. It is like oil in a car. A little will get you started, but you need more to keep you going. If you run without it, you will soon suffer a breakdown.

The Rejected Reject

Rejection is defined as the act of being rejected. To be rejected is to be unaccepted, unacknowledged, or pushed aside. There are other words that more hideously describe rejection, such as abandon or deny.

There are many causes of rejection. Some are self-imposed. There are those who have been rejected for so long they have adapted a lifestyle of rejection, and the truth is they really fear acceptance. They learn not to intermingle with people. They become introverted and anti-social. They do and say things that cause people to reject them. There is always an interesting history behind people who reach this point. Most times it stems all the way back to their childhood. In all my years of counseling and ministering to those who are lonely, hurting, or rejected, if I've learned anything at all, I've learned that usually the rejected reject others. Sometimes they reject knowingly and other times they reject unknowingly. Many times our hurts will cause us to hurt others. I can relate back to my own personal experience of rejection after loss. About four years after Jerome's death, a young man and his family started attending our church. I'll refer to him as Chuck. Chuck and his wife first came to visit my wife and I for marriage counseling. Their marriage was failing. They had been separated and on the verge of divorce. We gave them some basic scripture guidelines and personal experience testimonies and within two or three weeks their marriage seemed to be coming back together again. They eventually joined our church and accepted us as their spiritual parents. At this stage in my life I had an immense need to feel like a father. My own sons seemed to be pre-occupied with their own dreams and desires. I didn't know how to tell them I needed them. The truth of the matter is I needed them to need me. I wanted them to seek my advice and counsel the way others had. I wanted to be a part in their growing into manhood and making the right decisions. I tried so hard to communicate to them how much I needed them. After awhile I began to feel like it was too late, so I stopped trying. I felt I should have built a better relationship with them when they were younger, then they would be able to communicate with me now.

My wife was a big help to me. She was always close to our sons and could talk to them, and they to her, about almost anything. I asked her, "Why are my sons so distant from me? Why is it teens from all the places I've gone to minister, can call me and seek my advice and counsel? They say I'm easy to talk to and they can relate to me about things they could never talk to their own parents about. Why can't I have the same effect on my own children? I am a nice person." My wife looked at me and said, "Honey, it's your approach." You've always tried to teach them to respect you as a father and the head of the house. In doing so, you've instilled fear instead. Do you remember when one of your spiritual daughters called you from Canada and she was drunk? As she cried and poured her heart out to you over the phone, you responded in a gentle fatherly tone. You said, "Sweetheart it's going to be all right. I understand that your parents are separating and you're feeling at a loss for direction, but drinking is not the answer." "On the other hand," she continued, "when your own son came home drunk one night for the first time, you yelled at the top of your lungs and there was almost a fistfight. Your approach was totally different in dealing with your own son, therefore his response is different. It was a hard pill to swallow, but I had to admit my wife was right. Most of our behavior is learned behavior. When my first son came from my wife's womb, there were no instructions with him. Almost everything you get that's new comes with an instruction manual or user's guide. My first child came when I was not more than a child myself, at 18 years old. Instinct lead me to raise my children the way my dad raised me. My dad was the boss in our house. If he made a decision he never asked me what I thought about it. I remember some joyful times I shared with my dad as we went fishing or just did household things together, but I never remember being able to express myself. I never remember being able to just sit and talk with my dad as I often did with my mom. Now, I know rejection can often stem from lack of communication. One of the most important and valuable gifts a parent can give their children is communication. Children need to be able to communicate without fear of retaliation or rejection. The task of parents is to teach children to maintain a level of respect for them as adults, and the authority figures of their families.

At a time in my life when I felt like I had failed as a father, Chuck shows up. As my counsel brought him and his wife closer, his need for a father brought him and I closer. He began to call me dad, and I called him son. He would call me everyday if I didn't call him first. He was very athletic and we would work out a lot at the gym together. We would often go bowling and best of all we would talk for hours. Every time he needed advice he would call me. I was living on a cloud. I felt like God had given me a second chance. He was so much like Jerome. He was even the same age as Jerome would have been, had he been alive. It came to the point I favored Chuck above my own sons. It was like a dream come true.

Everything I wanted in a son I found in Chuck. I was totally consumed with the idea of playing the role of a father. I had been through so much hurt and pain, I was beginning to feel like what was happening to me was too good to be true. I woke up many days wondering when destruction would hit my world and things would fall apart again. Negative grief has a way of entrapping its victims into a cycle of hopelessness. It's like the person who has been sick for so long they have forgotten what being well feels like. They adapt the feeling of sickness as a way of life. If the person woke up one morning feeling well, they would think something was wrong. Many times when I was with Chuck I would say to him, "I know someday you are going to leave. You'll probably move back east and be closer to your real father." He would then say, "Dad, I could never leave you; you just don't know how much you mean to me. I've never been this close to my real father, but I can talk to you about anything."

Apostle Eugene Satterwhite Th.D.

For Father's Day, Chuck gave me a cup that read, "Anyone can be a father, but it takes a special person to be a Dad." He would always say what I wanted or needed to hear. Within a few weeks I unknowingly slipped back into a fantasy world of denial. I began to believe God somehow had really made him my son to replace Jerome. I began to treat him like I always wanted to treat Jerome and do for him what I never had a chance to do for Jerome. As a matter of fact every time I called his name with my mouth, I said Chuck, but with my heart I said Jerome.

Then like Job said, "The thing I feared came upon me." All of a sudden things changed and circumstances caused him to have to move. He moved closer to his wife's parents. All of a sudden, I felt like I had been demoted from dad to dog. Chuck quit calling and refused to answer my calls. He made himself totally unavailable to me. "What did I do?" I thought. "Where did I go wrong?" I had never in my life felt such rejection. My hurt turned to anger and my anger turned to rage. At one point, I thought I even wished him dead. I remember walking down on the waterfront near our house. Tears were streaming down my face, camouflaged by the rain. Then I realized what I was feeling was familiar. It was the same feeling I felt for Jerome's assailant. Grief then again began to lay claim on my life. I had to relive the pain of lost love. I started to resent the day I met Chuck. My mind told me to hate him, but my heart wouldn't cooperate. I felt melancholy inside. Depression drove me to compulsive eating, and eating kept me depressed. I purposed in my heart never to be close to anyone again. Because of the rejection I felt, I began to reject those that really loved me. It's astonishing how we can focus so much on our losses that we often forget what we still have. I had other natural and spiritual sons and daughters that needed me as much as I needed them, but hurt and rejection blinded my eyes to everything else that was important in life. I had to really come to grips with myself. As I began to get back to the place of prayer God called me to, he again began to speak to my heart.

When the lights of my soul finally came on again, I then began to realize how selfish I had been. I never thought about what Chuck might have been going through. I was just concerned about what he was putting me through. I later learned his wife had been diagnosed with cancer, his marriage was failing, and he had lost interest in Jesus and the church. He reverted back to his old ways and he didn't want anything to do with a preacher, even if his name was 'Dad.' I began to understand it was Jesus he was rejecting, not me. This new understanding made it easier to live with the loss but it didn't ease the pain. Once again I had to trust God to remove the hurt and bring healing. God has taught me the first step toward ending rejection is self-acceptance. If you can love yourself, then you can love others. The love you give will return to you in the end.

Apostle Eugene Satterwhite Th.D.

Pass the Grief

When my grandmother died, I had a very puzzling encounter with grief. My brothers, sisters, and I grew up in Texas. They lived in San Antonio and I lived partially with my grandmother in a nearby town called Wielder, Texas. During this time I became very close to my grandmother who we called 'Mommy.' When I got word mommy had died, I felt a feeling of sadness, but I didn't break down and cry. We were living in Washington State at the time. Some of the family members were able to fly home for the funeral. Then I was asked to officiate the funeral, "How could I?" were my thoughts. I tried to get out of it, but the family decided I was the one for the job since I was the only pastor and ordained minister in the family at the time. My father's persuasion compelled me to accept. He said it would be an honor to have his son honor his mom at death. I accepted a job I didn't think I could handle. It was inconceivable how I was able to go through with the funeral and not break down one single time. I didn't understand what was happening. "Why am I not falling apart? Why can't I grieve like everyone else? It can't be because I don't love her. I loved her like a mother." While everyone else was grieving I felt like saying, "Pass the grief." I tried to even make myself cry, but couldn't. At her funeral I prayed, I sang, and I preached, but I never cried. Two years later I drove to Texas with a friend for a convention in which I was the main speaker. I had some extra time so we decided to drive to Wielder and visit the house where mommy had lived. When we pulled up in front of the house and I looked at the old rocker she used to sit in, it seemed like a fountain full of tears burst from within me. All the pain and grief of her death that somehow had been locked up inside me came forth like a volcanic eruption. I couldn't even get out of the car. I just sat there and cried. The person who was traveling with me was totally confounded. My mommy had died two years ago, and I was responding like it was two seconds ago. Reality had to be affirmed. I received the message of her death two years ago and preached the funeral, but the reality of it didn't hit home until then.

Then I began to understand what had happened. Since mommy was so far away, I only saw her occasionally when I went to Texas. She was always there when I needed her. Seeing her was always the highlight of my trip. That was my first trip back to Texas since she had died. Even when we went to her funeral I was able to sit with 'Mommy' at the funeral home after they had prepared her body. But two years later, for the first time in my life, I went to mommy's home to see her, only to find her not there. It was then, and only then, I came to the realization I would never see her again in this life.

There are also ways we can prolong our grieving process. Along with unforgiveness, there's unacceptance. The longer it takes one to accept what has happened, the longer it will take one to deal with the grief. In the case of my grandmother, maybe if I had gone back to the house after the funeral and spent some quiet time there I may have gotten relief from the grief sooner. Instead I chose to stay busy preparing for her funeral and blocked out the reality of mommy's death.

This brings to mind the controversial belief one should stay busy when they are experiencing grief or loss to help take their mind off of things. On the other hand, there are the those who say you should sit and relax and let others handle the important affairs. Well, I'm here to tell you from personal experience neither way sets precedence about how one should behave during the grieving period. For some, keeping busy is the best therapy for grief. Others need to just get plenty of rest. An important prerequisite for those who are grieving is to release their emotions. That may mean putting everything on hold and taking a few moments for you to ponder what has happened and begin to accept the reality of it. I've known people to go into a state of shock when they have heard of the death of a loved one and they stayed in that for months after the funeral. When reality finally surfaced, they had a nervous breakdown.

Apostle Eugene Satterwhite Th.D.

Let Us Move On To Perfection

The worm like caterpillar,
Awaits her appointed time.
To perfect into a butterfly,
Leaving the past behind.

A lifeless seed is planted,
Awaiting nature's given hour.
To spring forth from soil of earth,
And blossom into a flower.

And we God's chosen people,
Should likewise show progress.
As living epistles, read of men,
Bringing life to what we confess.

Not fighting the same old battles,
And covering the same lost ground.
The bondage of yesterday,
Today still holds some bound.

Days go by, months they fly,
Yet no signs of the abundant life.
Many have walked with God for years,
And have never won a soul for Christ.

The gardener looks on his vineyard,
For fresh fruit to enjoy.
The husband searches his field,
For a willing heart to employ.

How sad when he's searched diligently,
And these he cannot obtain.
Though given much care and pruning,
Or lives remain the same.

So let us move on to perfection,
Set higher goals than ever.
Add excellence to our effort,
And endurance to our endeavor.

Oh let's move on to perfection,
Not settling for second best.
Suppressing those foes of Satan,
Turning defeats to success.

Oh come! Move on to perfection,
To enjoy the blessing it holds.
Only those who attempt the impossible,
Shall achieve incredible goals.

Apostle Eugene Satterwhite Th.D.

The Love Connection

There are very few alcoholics who didn't gag at their first taste of alcohol. Just as there are few chain smokers that didn't gag or cough when they took their very first puff. Habits will cause us to cleave to what we once hated. Once you've done it for so long, it soon becomes a way of life. I discovered in my counseling of those suffering from grief, it is possible to become addicted. Grief is not a terrible thing. It has some positive affects on many people. It is something everyone must face sooner or later in life. It can make us stronger, happier people. It can help us find ourselves and discover who we really are.

Though it can have all these positive affects on us, it was not intended to be adapted as a way of life. Some people have carried grief so long they have become addicted. The painful emotions they once despised, they now crave. Most addictions are based on a feeling the substance gives them rather than the substance itself. Whether it's the alcoholic's high, or the so-called "soothing rush" from a crack pipe, it's all a feeling. Those that use grief as their narcotic, to get them high, are those who refuse to let go. They have grown to like the feeling of sorrow. Maybe it's because of all the attention they get. There are those who felt unimportant until they suffered grief, and then they became the focus of everyone's attention. Although it wasn't worth the pain I felt, and could never replace the loss, I must confess I did enjoy the special attention I received during my bereavement time. There were cards and telegrams from all over the world, the phone was ringing off the hook, and flowers and finances were sent. I felt like a celebrity. Calls came from bishops and important men I didn't even knew existed. I can easily see how a person can get hooked on these feelings. But like everything else, it is still temporal. One thing we must remember, it is after the attention goes away that the bereaved will need help and comfort. After the minister has gone, after relatives have gone home, after the cards stop coming, and the phone stops ringing. This is the time that a grieving person needs a friend who will be there no matter what. Someone who will listen, even if what they are saying makes little sense.

I have a friend who worked the graveyard shift at a local grocery store. Many times when I couldn't sleep at night, I would go and visit with him. He didn't talk much, but he was a good listener. The funny thing about it is he wasn't even professing to be a Christian at the time. Yet, he was the greatest help to me. This goes to show you don't have to be a pastor, evangelist, or great Bible scholar to minister to hurting hearts. All you need is an available caring heart and a listening ear.

I often wonder why people in abusive relationships will many times go back to their abusers. I once read a newspaper article that had a title that read: "Better Divorced Than Dead." It was a heartbreaking story. A housewife had been in and out of a homeless shelter for battered women. The man that ran the shelter tried to no avail to get the woman to stay away from her violent, physically abusive husband. The church she attended didn't believe in divorce for any reason at all. It's marriage until "death do you part" no matter what. The pastor, along with members of the congregation, would always encourage her to go back home and try to work things out with her husband. She would always go back and each time the beatings would get more severe. I am not an advocate for divorce, but I agree with the writer of the article, "Better Divorced Than Dead." What makes a person go back for more? Do they like the pain? What gratification do they get from being hurt and abused? I found many people who return to their abusive relationships are love addicts. They are addicted to love. They have to have love or at least feel like they have it. In my experience in counseling, I've found that much of this behavior comes from low self-esteem. Many times the victim feels they deserve to be abused. They believe if they were different their companion wouldn't have to lose their temper and go off. This is a lie. Nobody has a right to abuse another person for any reason at all. Many times a woman may crave that warm feeling of so called "love and acceptance"

Apostle Eugene Satterwhite Th.D.

during the making up times, so she will stay in a relationship just for that feeling. Her abuser may feel guilty and ashamed and try to compensate by giving her flowers and expensive gifts. Others may enjoy the feeling of having him beg for their forgiveness. For once in their relationship the woman feels like she is in control. The wife can call the shots. The husband is completely at her mercy. Although she knows within herself he will do it again, she still returns to him, just for the feeling.

Most of our bad habits are obtained through learned behavior and can be quite addictive. To break loose we must understand healthy positive decisions and action merit reward. If the only reward for giving and doing in a relationship is detrimental to your well-being, then you should seek counsel for both of you, or end the relationship. You must develop enough self-worth to know you don't deserve to be abused.

Every addiction or habit that is broken must be replaced by something. Whether it will be replaced by something more positive or more negative than itself. If you are addicted to love, then you should learn to love yourself enough to protect yourself from abuse.

Love Faileth Not

When you have been mistreated,
Revenge might cross your mind.

You should try to shun hard feelings,
But contentment you can't find.

You spend many sleepless nights,
Trying to forget.

You pray for God's assistance,
But find no answer yet.

Well, God left us a remedy,
In case you forgot.

The bible plainly lets us know,
That love faileth not.

Love will cover all the faults,
In others we might see.

For a spirit of forgiving,
It's the perfect receipt.

Although you smile at others,
And only get a frown.

Love will melt that stony heart,
And bring those high minds down.

Apostle Eugene Satterwhite Th.D.

They won't know you by faith,
Though you may have a lot.

They'll know you're a Christian by your love,
For love faileth not.

Who's To Blame

Since the fall of man it has been the Adamic nature of man to pass the blame. When Adam sinned, God asked Adam, "Where art thou?" God wasn't playing hide and seek with Adam. God knew exactly where Adam was and what he had done. God wanted a confession and repentance. When God asked Adam if he had eaten of the tree, Adam passed the blame to the woman. He said in *Genesis 3:12, "The woman thou gavest to be with me, she gave me of the tree, and I did eat."* In other words, he was saying, "It is the woman's fault for giving it to me and it is God's fault for giving me the woman." When God questioned the woman, she blamed the serpent. Today when we fail God and walk in rebellion, we often blame it on the devil. We say, "The devil made me do it." Well, the devil may have been there to influence you, but his influence for you to do wrong was no greater than the influence of the Holy Spirit for you to do right. The final choice is up to you, since it is you who will reap the consequences of your decision.

I have learned when I am faced with temptation, I do not just merely try to resist. The bible doesn't teach us to resist, it teaches us to flee temptation. Joseph fled from the Potters wife and maintained his integrity. David did not flee and fell into sin. I can't imagine standing over a naked woman trying to resist. I must flee. Joseph had a perfect opportunity to excuse or justify his sin with his ruler's wife. He was away from home, and no one had to know. Joseph had been abused and forsaken by those he loved. He was grieving from loss of love and family. Yet he did not even dwell on the thought of yielding. He simply fled. Those who are experiencing grief and loss must be very careful not to use their condition as an excuse for failure. They must be watchful because they are in a very vulnerable state. Many times during grieving periods we let our defenses down. We may start breaking rules and standards we had set to govern our lives. You may get to where you don't care what people think about you.

You start thinking they should understand your failure because of what you have dealt with. After all you are only human. If there was ever a time I felt comfortable with failure, it was when I was grieving. The devil would tell me to take a drink or do some drugs. No one will know, and if they do find out they will understand you are just going through a phase in your life. They will say it will pass and you will again be that strong, vigilant man of God you were before tragedy hit. On the contrary, the Bible teaches us in *Proverbs 24:10, "If thou faint in the day of adversity, thy strength is small."* Therefore, the true test of my character is in the way I handle adversity. I am therefore no greater than my ability to endure hardships. Most of the great men in the bible are noted for their attitude and behavior. Shadrach, Meshach, and Abednego have had some great administrative skills in order to hold such high offices in the King's court. They are remembered most because of the fiery furnace. Daniel was a prophet and a dream interpreter, yet the first thing that comes to mind when we think of Daniel is the lion's den. I've known people who claimed to be atheists, after watching me go through all that I went through, tell me they were convinced I had something they did not have.

All the prior preaching, teaching, witnessing, and good deeds I had done to win them was to no avail. It took my fiery furnace experience to convince them there is a God who can sustain you no matter what you face. During those dark hours of my life, I adopted a testimony from David in *Psalms 71:18, "Now when I am old and grey-headed, Oh God, forsake me not; until I have showed thy strength unto this generation, and thy power to everyone that is to come."*

We are living in a generation of scoffers who have seen the fall of many great men of God. They have seen the negative side of the church. They have seen hypocrisy. I want to show them the positive side. I want to show God's power and demonstrate his ability to keep his church. I want to show them that not every preacher is out to take their money or go to bed with the first woman that avails herself. I want to show these nonbelievers there are men who truly love God, and will not bow down to Satan's images. The world will never stop pointing the finger at the church, but now they'll point to something positive. I once lived in a community that had at least 42 churches and only 6 gangs. The gangs seemingly always made the news, while the churches remained in the background. According to statistics, there are more Christians than gang members. Christians are the one's who will make the headlines, as we show God's strength to this generation.

Blaming yourself, God, and others is a part of the grief process most people will face, especially when it involves a death that could have been prevented. Look at what Martha said to Jesus after her brother Lazarus died, *"Then said Martha unto Jesus, Lord, if thou had been here, my brother had not died," St. John 11:21.* How many times in life have you experienced people blaming family or friends for not being there? Perhaps, you had to deal with guilt or self- condemnation because you weren't there. I remember an incident in my life when a young man I knew as a friend came to a service where I was ministering. He had been drinking heavily. He wanted to talk to me, but I was busy with other people. Finally I went and told the young man where I was staying so he could set a time to meet with me privately. The next night he came back to the church again. He had been drinking again. He didn't come inside the church. As I was leaving he beckoned me over to his car and handed me a note. I put the letter in my pocket. Later I transferred the letter to my briefcase, where I totally forgot about it. Just a short time after our brief encounter, I was called upon to preach this young man's funeral. He had committed suicide.

This was one of the most difficult funerals I've ever had to officiate. He was my close friend, he was so young, so handsome, and so gifted. How could he commit suicide? He had so much to live for. Why did he choose to end it all? Whenever there is a suicide, there is always room to pass the blame. Family members may blame each other. They may blame friends, the medics, or the police for not responding faster.

In this case I, too, was blamed. I was told the night before his death, the young man was trying desperately to reach me. I was ministering out of town. Although I felt guilt for not being there for him, I wasn't going to take the blame for his death. Six months later when I was going through some old notes, I found the note the young man had handed me that night at the church. It hadn't been opened. It had gotten mixed up with some of my notes and I never thought about it again until that day. I was devastated. I could hear his cry for help. He was reaching out for me, but I wasn't there. As I continued to read the letter I could see desperation in his words, as they seemed to leap from the note to grasp my bleeding heart. He poured his heart out to me and I turned my back. I felt sick inside. I felt like a murderer. I had the power to save a life, but I didn't use it. How could I live with myself? I became my own prosecutor, judge, and jury. I sentenced myself to life in a prison of guilt and remorse. I feasted on condemnation and despair. I needed to be set free again, from this self-constructed prison of the mind.

I again had to turn to God for deliverance. Through fasting and prayer and the foundation of the word of God, I found freedom from this guilt. God allowed me to see I am only accountable for what I know. *James 4:17, "Therefore to him that knoweth to do good, and doth it not, to him it is sin."* I did not know the state of mind my friend was in. I had begun to think on all the times I was there for him. There were many nights I did spend trying to help him work through his problems. I even invited him to come and live at my house for a season so he could get strong and break the ties of bad associations. If he had talked to me the night before or even if I'd been there the night he committed suicide, who's to say he would not have still carried out his plan. He had talked about suicide in the past. Maybe by being there I would have just prolonged the inevitable. Many times those that handle the blame are not strong enough to handle the guilt that accompanies it. From this experience, I concluded my life could no longer be based on what others do. I am to take the blame for my actions alone. It is my duty to point my brothers in the right direction, but their decision or the consequences of their decision is on the person.

Apostle Eugene Satterwhite Th.D.

Forgive And Live

So you've been hurt or wounded,
By thoughtless word and deed.

The inward scars are painful,
They cause the heart to bleed.

You feel you don't deserve this,
From one you've loved so dear,

No band-aid can help you,
No medicine, it's too severe.

Don't bury the hurts within you,
They only work to kill.

Unless you release forgiveness,
No pain time can heal.

Most of all our sicknesses,
Are caused by the roots of unforgiveness.

Let not bitterness steal your health,
Or hatred cause your death.

The Woman Thou Gaveth Me

The blaming stage of grief for my wife, Joy and me, was the most difficult. We blamed the ministry, the members, even the mechanic that made us late when we were supposed to pick up our son. Worst of all we blamed each other. I remember sitting and racking my brain with all the "what if." What if she had done this, or if I hadn't done that; maybe he would still be alive today. Accusations lead to condemnation, which almost lead to separation. Our harsh and piercing words to each other made it impossible to live together. Once we ran out of reasons to blame each other, we turned the blame to God. We told ourselves, "God did this to us. He may as well have pulled the trigger." It was all a lie from Satan. Satan's strategy was to get us angry with God, and to turn our backs on our only true source of help for deliverance and healing.

The grief process taught me so much about the woman he had given me. I realize how little I knew about my wife's emotions and sensitivity to issues. I discovered the real depth of a mother's love for her children. When there is a divorce or separation it is generally the mother who will keep the children, while the father goes on about his business. When a mother has carried a seed inside of her for nine months, she watched the seed grow as her body changes dimensions. Lastly, the mother goes through caustic labor pains that are in many cases life threatening. After nine months, I do not feel most Godly women are eager to walk away from their babies. The things which you have paid a great price for, you tend to cleave to. My wife had a special attachment to our son Jerome, because there was so much about him that reminded her of me. He'd tell her to go to bed when I was away. He wanted to make sure she got her rest. If she had to be out at night he would stay up until she came home. My wife developed a binding relationship with him.

When she lost him, it seemed like her world had fallen apart. She seemed to shut me and everybody who cared for her out.

We started drifting apart. We were no longer intimate. I felt like a stove that was married to a refrigerator, who was becoming a freezer. Our marriage needed help. One day I said to her, "I don't know what you want from me. I cook, I help with housework, and I provide a good living for you. Now, what do you want?" Joy caustically added, "You mean to tell me that you can pray for dozens of people in prayer lines at church and get a word of direction for their lives, but God can't tell you how to meet the spiritual and emotional needs of your own wife?" I opened my mouth to respond but nothing came out. I tried to think of a rebuttal, but found none. It was a hard pill to swallow, but I had to take it for what it was worth. I had been insensitive to her feelings as a woman. One thing I learned that I will never forget is everyone has a right to his or her own feelings. If a person feels a certain way about a certain thing, then that's their right. The situation may not be the way it is perceived, but if the person feels a certain way then to them that's the way it is. We should respect their feelings. Where I used to pray and ask God to show Joy where she was wrong, I now pray and ask him what I can do to make my wife feel differently. If Joy feels differently she'll respond differently. Things did not change overnight. I had to really seek God for some answers. Not all marriages could stand the test that ours had to stand. Some marriages fail because the husband and wife do not want to face reality. I pray our lives will serve as a testimony of strength for those who have suffered the loss of a loved one.

My needs were automaticlly met when I stopped being selfish and focused on my wife's needs. I had to learn about nonverbal communication. I had to learn to say I love you, without words. Sometimes with flowers or a gift, when it wasn't even her birthday. Many times as men we get in trouble by not being concerned about the emotions of our wives. Our wives expect us to pick up without having to come out and say it. There are times when my wife has had to tell me something after the fact. I would say to her, "Why didn't you just say so from the beginning?" she'd say, "That's what I've been trying to tell you." Then I'd say, "Well, why didn't you just say it plainly, so I could understand?" My wife's response was, "If you don't know me by now, too bad." Remember men, by the time our wives have to tell it, it's already too late.

In order to meet the needs of a woman you have to know what their needs are. I thought I knew Joy, but I didn't. I was trying to meet a need she really didn't have. To my surprise, I had to face the fact sex was not at the top of a woman's list of priorities in marriage nor was it my wife's priority. Sex had become a way of escape for me. After all the things I had encountered during this period of time sex had become a way of escape from reality. The world seemed to let me down. Everywhere I turned there seemed only to be negativity. There was one place I felt where I could turn to find relief and that was in bed with my wife. I would forget my cares and frustration and bury my pain with sexual fulfillment. Sex to me was like crack cocaine to a drug addict or wine to the alcoholic. It was my way of escape from reality. All the while, my wife was aware of what was going on which contributed to her withdrawal from me. Many nights I would still be angry, frustrated, and depressed about everything, until I received sexual fulfillment. I'd awake with a whole new outlook on my situation. On the other hand, my wife would wake up the next day with an even greater feeling of depression. When a person feels like they are being used it is hard to participate in something you like or should enjoy. I like ministering to people, but if I start feeling like I am being used and not appreciated, then it makes my job as a minister less desirable to me. I have to remind myself I am ministering for God.

When I took a good look at myself, I began to cry out to God for deliverance from this addiction that was destroying my marriage and ruining my life. God was no longer my top priority. I needed to make a love connection first with God and then the spirit and soul of my wife and not just her body. I had put her through double jeopardy. Not only did Joy have to deal with the loss of a son, but an immature, insensitive husband who only cared about making himself look and feel good. These things are hard and embarrassing to admit, but if my life's testimony is to be effective to those who are hurting, then it must be told in its entirety. There are countless numbers of men who are full of pride that won't let themselves admit they were and are wrong. Who may stumble across this book. I pray that you will find yourself here and do what I have done. I repented to God and to my wife. I had to learn what it really meant to be a husband and the head of my household.

    I am now learning how to love my wife as Christ loves her, and to be what Christ is to the church. When I was younger, I used to think when we first got married, I could keep my wife satisfied by keeping a physically attractive body. I spent hours in the gym working out daily, trying to maintain my figure. After years of bodybuilding, I found out another thing about the woman God gave me. If all she wanted me for, in the first place, was my physique, then I was in trouble from the very beginning of our relationship. No matter how good you look, there is always someone who looks better than you. I couldn't compete with all that competition. I found out when you have a woman who really loves God, such as I have, then the best way to win her affection is to get closer to God. Who can compete with God? I discovered the level of my intimacy with God will determine the level of intimacy with my wife. God will turn her heart toward me. *"And thy desire shall be to thy husband..." Genesis 3:16.*

Overcoming "Triple A" / Anger, Attitude, and Anxiety

There are other great hurdles to cross in the grief process – anger, attitude, and anxiety. First, we must deal with anger. Remember these are all a part of our God given emotions. Everyone has them, no one is exempt. Anger can be channeled through our lives as a fruit-producing asset, or as a devastating liability. Many people are unaware anger is the root cause of their problems; everything else is superficial. Many of the fires of various addictions are lit by sparks of anger. If a man that was addicted to drugs can maintain his freedom from drugs when he is in anger, then he is truly delivered. I find many people who have bad habits or addictions can control then until they get angry enough. Anger will cause you to go back to drinking, smoking, fornicating, stealing, lying, wife abuse, child abuse or whatever else you were used to doing.

A person may become a passive aggressive person with their anger. This type of a person is one who holds his true feelings inside until they push the wrong button. For example, when a person's boss tells him to do something he doesn't agree with, he may give you a unsincere smile and say "yes sir." But under his breath he is saying, "You are so stupid, that's not the way it should be done." Passive aggressive people have some concern about the feelings of others. They are careful not to let their attitude get in the way of their jobs. When a person reaches the stage of rage, that is the "I don't care stage." That's why some people will never tell you what they are really feeling until they reach a point of rage. They lose control of reality. They have no regard for who you are or what your position is. Rage will make them tell you just what they think of you. When I see all the tragedy around the world, I wonder what makes people behave the way they do. It is rage. Look at the teenager in Washington State that walked into the classroom with a gun and opened fire on his fellow students and teacher. Look at the man who walked into a restaurant in Texas and began shooting innocent strangers. Consider the man who walked into his house and began shooting his wife and children, and then turned the gun on himself. Was it just anger that caused these people to act with such violent behavior or was it rage? I believe it was rage.

I found out that in the grief process, I had to deal with the anger that was quickly turning to rage. I needed a change of attitude. Two weeks before my son died, I felt like I could conquer any demon from hell. I had put so much confidence in my flesh. I had just ended a 31 day fast and was on the mountaintop. I felt like I was ready for just about anything. Then my son was murdered. I made it through the funeral just fine. But after the funeral was over, the cards were all read, and the phone stopped ringing, that's when my wife and I needed a real friend. Remember, when you are trying to minister to a person who has lost a loved one, it is usually shortly after the funeral when they need you most. That's when the real battle begins in their mind. It was hard for me to have negative thoughts, when people were saying positive things to me. But, when friends had gone home and no one was there to encourage me, that's when my integrity was really tested. Two weeks after the death of my son, I went into a battle of the mind with Satan that almost put me on the streets and on crack cocaine. The Holy Spirit came to remind me of the miracle God had performed through my prayers or laying on of hands. I was reminded of a girl in Canada whose skull was cracked, and through my prayers, God put it back together again. The doctors had two sets of x-rays, one with a cracked skull, and one after I had prayed, with a fully restored skull. I was reminded of the cancers that God had healed, of the woman that God grew inches on her leg, and the little boy who the doctor said would never walk again because of a bone deteriorating disease. Through my prayers, God not only stopped deterioration but he caused new bone tissue to grow.

"But when you need God the most," Satan reminded me, "he turned his back on you." You may as well go and take some crack. They said once you get hooked you don't care about anything else but more crack. Jesus is the only one who can replace that feeling and give you a spiritual high. Since the devil had now almost totally convinced me Jesus was against me, I felt my only relief had to be crack. For weeks I went through intense warfare, battling an urge I never had before. I wanted to display my anger toward God by using cocaine. I thank God for the victory. Praise God, I never did have to turn to crack or alcohol for relief from this pain of grief. God sent a revival to town. There was a woman by the name of Mother Stella Boyd. I had heard about this powerful woman, but never had the chance to meet her until this time in my life when I needed a great deliverance. When Mother Boyd prayed for me, it was like a great burden was lifted. I discovered something else happened that night. The Lord, through this mother, had birthed within me a tremendous gift to write praise and worship songs. I have always loved and written poetry and song, but never before were such songs birthed in my spirit as after this great night of my deliverance. One of the first songs that came forth from my spirit was.

Holy Ghost Anointing

Holy Ghost anointing
Fall afresh on me
Holy Ghost anointing
Renew your presence in me

Oh let the fire from heaven
Burn out all my sins
Let thy living water over me pour
Take out all the wrong
And place your righteousness within
Bread of heaven feed me till I want no more
Bread of heaven feed me till I want no more

Apostle Eugene Satterwhite Th.D.

The anxiety that caused my anger had also changed my attitude. The new songs gave me a new attitude. I had to overcome with an attitude of gratitude. Instead of accusing God I was praising Him. Now I could see through the eyes of hope and not despair. I learned what it really meant to be thankful to God. There are a lot of people going through the routine of what they call praise to God, but they are not at all thankful. Your thankfulness shows up in your attitude. You can praise God and not be thankful, but you can't be thankful and not praise God. Thankfulness demands praise. Praise strengthens my faith in Christ and leaves no place for anxiety. When negative traits catch hold of your attitude, they get on a roll. Anxiety causes anger, anger causes sin, sin causes guilt, and guilt causes depression. You must stop the cycle with a change of attitude.

After I was delivered from the anger stages of my grief, I could clearly see my own error. Anger has a way of blinding us from the truth so we can't see ourselves the way we really are. I once prayed a prayer in anger and that prayer was answered. I did what a parent should never do. I gave up on my son. He had caused me so much hurt and pain, I gave up on him. I prayed to God and said, "Lord whatever it takes, I just want to see Jerome saved?" Well, my prayer was answered about a year later. On his deathbed as I ministered to him, he accepted Christ as his Savior. Through my experience I found out there are four things you should not do when you get angry:

1) Make major decisions.

When you are angry, you are not in the right frame of mind to be making major decisions. Many people have quit their jobs, sold their cars, left their churches, and broken off relationships in their moment of anger. Some decisions can be repaired after you come to your senses but others can never be corrected. Take, for example, a woman who found out her husband had an affair. She got angry and decided she would do likewise. Well, the woman ended up pregnant, she lost her husband, her lover, and was left with an illegitimate child to raise. All because she got angry and made a bad decision in her stage of anger.

2) Never spank your children when angry.

Our emotions can cause an increase of adrenaline, which can enable us to do things that normally are impossible. I once heard of a mother that was in a car accident with her baby who was pinned under the car. Without even thinking, she rushed over and with seemingly supernatural strength, she lifted the car to free her baby. That same adrenaline rises when we get excessively angry. When you spank your children while you are angry, you may be using more force than you realize.

3) Never use drugs, alcohol, food or sex as an outlet.

Anger does not mix with any of these things. It will only lead to more depression or violent behavior.

4) Never minister, counsel, or teach others when you are angry.

Although you may try to hide your anger, it will surface as you try to teach or minister to others. Your ideas will often be one sided and you most likely won't have an open mind.

It is God's desire to see every Christian clothed with the garment of praise, and not with anger. We can defeat every foe and conquer every enemy if we just go to God for an attitude adjustment. We can take back lost ground if we stay focused on what God can do rather than what has happened to us or who hurt us.

Apostle Eugene Satterwhite Th.D.

Living With Losses and Loving Life

Loss, in a sense, is a way of life. Everyone has to face losses in their lives. Some losses are necessary losses, and some are not. We have to suffer the loss of sunshine to get the much-needed rain. People die and others are born. In the book of Ecclesiastes, chapter 13, the bible teaches there is a time for every purpose under the heaven.

Our time of loss of a human being seems to be the most difficult. There are some things we want to get rid of. There are things we lose by giving them away. In many cases loss means change and change is something we really don't like doing. In many cases we have to adjust our lifestyles to the loss. Many times we have to face life after losing that which we never thought we could live without. The things that are close to our hearts that we lose can sometimes leave an irreplaceable void. When you have cleaved to something for a long time, you often feel lost without it. When many older couples I know have been married for years, and one of them dies, I have noticed it is not long before the other will follow. Some say they grieve themselves to death. It may be they just gave up on life. I found out in many cases when you give up on life, life gives up on you. There are those who have been told they have a terminal disease and only have a short time to live. Through a strong will to live, they overcome their sickness and out live others that were healthier.

The way a loss occurs can also affect the way we deal with it. We tend to have a different attitude about a loved one that was lost through an auto accident or loss of material or irreplaceable possessions by a fire, than if they had been murdered. Material things I have worked for, I would rather lose or have destroyed in an accident rather than have someone steal them from me. Nothing makes me angrier than having things stolen from me. That can lead to rage. One of our neighbors who had been robbed several times got so angry he went out, bought a shot gun and vowed to shoot anyone who came near his garage again. This is an example of rage. When someone murders a loved one, they rob you in the worst way. I felt like the man that murdered my son had taken a part of me. He might as well have shot me too. He robbed me of years of happiness. He robbed me of my unborn grandchildren my son could have produced. It is hard to believe one deed, one small handgun, and one bullet could alter the course of my life forever. My son's untimely death is something that can never be undone. A person may steal a car or some material thing that can always be returned or replaced, but human life can never be replaced. Not any amount of money can compensate for the loss of a human life.

In another chapter of the story of my life, I remember getting what I wanted, but losing what I had. I always wanted a motorcycle but could never afford one. With growing kids to feed, it took all I had just to keep a good car running. One day a friend of mine gave me the motorcycle he had which had been sitting around for years. He seldom rode it, and he knew of my great desire to own a bike, so he gave me his. In my excitement, I went to pick up the bike immediately. I didn't consider I didn't have a license to drive the bike, nor did the bike have a registration or current tabs. I just rode the bike as it was. As I pulled into my yard, two motorcycle cops pulled in behind me. I got four tickets. The tickets caused my insurance premium to increase. The company I was insured through wanted to double my rates because of the tickets. So I canceled my policy with them. A few days later before I could find a lower insurance rate, my two cars were hit by a hit and run driver. I had a late model Audi 5000 I had purchased. I also had a second car, which was an older but good running Mercury. Both cars were parked in front of our house when our doorbell rang at about three o'clock in the morning. It was the police. They informed us that both our cars had been hit by a hit and run driver. When I looked at the cars I wanted to explode. They both were completely totaled. After I got my emotions under control I remembered I didn't even have insurance. That meant unless the police found the hit and run driver and he had insurance, then I was up a creek without a paddle. About 17 thousand dollars went down the drain. I cried myself to sleep that night.

The next day, I was so grieved over the loss of my cars all I could do was walk. I walked and cried. I questioned God, "Why?" I have given myself to serve people. "What did I do to deserve this?" These cars were not used to transport drugs or pick up prostitutes. They were used to carry the gospel to the lost and to pick people up and bring them to church. I've traveled many miles to Canada and Montana preaching on the Indian reservations. I was so angry with God for letting this happen to me. When I got home from my long walk, my wife, Joy, was full of smiles and praise. She was walking around the house acting like we had just won a sweepstakes. I said to her, "Do you know what has happened?" And she said, "Yes I know but I can't change what has happened so I might as well live with it and be happy." "If one of your special dishes got broken you'd be walking around like I am. Now when something major happens you act like it's no big deal." Joy responded, "Well, at least we are well balanced. You handle the big stuff and I'll handle the small stuff." I had to leave the house again. Grief has a way of making you want everyone to see things the way you do and feel exactly the way you feel. You hate to see people laughing when you are crying. You are very uncomfortable in a room full of people who are laughing when you are grieving inside.

I must say it was my wife's response to what happened that moved the hand of God. Her attitude caused God to come to our rescue. My harsh accusation took me further from God and from deliverance. Before the day had ended, a friend from out of town that owned a wrecking yard bought me another car. It was an older car than what I had, but it ran well and served me good until God gave me another new car.

By the time I went to bed that night, I was repenting to God. I had to again get an attitude adjustment. I had learned to praise

God and be thankful even when things go wrong. I concluded the easiest way to live with loss is to be thankful for what you still have.

Apostle Eugene Satterwhite Th.D.

Let Me Not Forget

Let me not forget
It's easier to remember you,
When all my needs aren't met.
But when showered with abundance,
How often I will forget.

I often claim my greed as need,
And taken your blessing for granted.
Your mercy has often caused me to reap,
Of seeds I had never planted.

Though prosperity be my lot,
Let graciousness always remain.
Keep me always in remembrance of Thee,
From whom all blessings came.

Lest I should lose all I've gained,
And at the very end regret.
Ever surround me with your love,
And let me not forget.

Handicapped By Hopelessness

In *St. John 5:1-14*, there is a story of a man which had an infirmity that disabled him from walking. He lay by a pool called Bethesda for thirty-eight long years waiting for the moving of the water, hoping that someday he would be first to enter the water after it was troubled by the angel. An angel would come down a certain season into the pool. Whoever stepped in first after troubling of the water was made whole of whatever disease he had. On this particular day, Jesus was in Jerusalem because there was a feast of the Jews going on. Instead of him being in the celebration ceremonies he wandered to a northern part of Jerusalem called Bethesda, where he found the man by the pool in a state of hopelessness. In this Lesson, I found seven reasons that cause hopelessness even in our lives today:

1) Your surrounding environment.

St. John 5:3 says, *"In these lay a great multitude of impotent folk, of blind, halt, withered, waiting for the moving of the water."* It is believed that many of the people who traveled to Jerusalem for the feast would bring their handicapped loved ones there and leave them at the pool while they enjoyed the feast. There was a larger than normal crowd of pool competitors during this time. As the lame man in our story looks around him, all he can see is people who are in the same or worse state as himself. They can't or won't help him. He can't help them. Your surrounding environment can create a spirit of hopelessness. It can affect the way you think. In many institutions great caution is used in the selection of color and scenery. You won't find dark gloomy colors on hospital walls. A person can change their outlook on life by changing their surroundings. I've known people to stay depressed by sitting around all day with the shades drawn. If you want light, then let some light in, take the depressing pictures off your walls. I found out as a black man, many or our so-called cultural pictures can have a negative effect on our spirit. Pictures of black people being oppressed can help keep the spirit of oppression alive. Try placing posters around your house filled with the word. Put one in every room. Fill your house with things that represent joy and life. Get some flowers and plants, so that everywhere you look there's life, not death. You may have to rid yourself of some old associates. If you have been getting counsel from someone who told you they are going through the same things you're going through, run for your life. They cannot pull you out of a ditch they have fallen into themselves.

2) The length of time.

St. John 5:5 says, *"And a certain man was there, which had infirmity thirty and eight years."* Many times the length of time we've had a condition, and not seen change, can create a spirit of hopelessness. Seemingly every time your hope is built up, it is only to be shot back down. You start to feel because things haven't changed yet, they never will. You start basing you future on your past. Your expectations change. You lose faith and start expecting things to go as they always have. You are now in Lodebar. The word "Lodebar," in the bible means destitute or deprived, without anything, without pasture. The place appears to have been situated beyond Jordan. It was probably the same as Deri or Lidbir. It was a place where the outcasts of society hung out. It was a place of great depression. It is mentioned in the bible in *Samuel, Chapter 9*. Jonathan had a son who lived there. After David became king, he sent for the son and brought him to live in this place as a tribute. His name was Mephibosheth, which means, destroying shame. He had been in Lodebar for so long he developed an attitude of no self esteem at all. Look at what he says when help finally came to bring him out of his situation: *"And he bowed himself, and said, What is they servant, that thou should look upon such a dead dog as I am?" 2 Samuel 9:9.* Deep depression will cause you to feel like you don't deserve the help you once hoped and prayed for. Mephibosheth had lost sight of who he was. His condition made him forget who he was. Many times our condition will make us, as believers, forget who we really are. Mephibosheth was the grandson of Saul who was king, which made him heir to the throne. David shouldn't have had to seek him out. He should have remembered the relationship David had with his father and then sought David for help. You are in a state of hopelessness when you refuse to seek the help that has been made available to you. Instead of seeking help, Mephibosheth meant 'destroy shame,' so he likened himself to something similar. A dog is one of the most shameless animals there is. He has no shame or standard about intercourse or where he has a bowel movement. He'll eat nearly anything that is given to him. When you start feeling like you have to take whatever life throws at you and are unwilling to change that which is in your ability to change, then you have adapted the dog mentality. Don't let time stagnate you. If you want to see a change, then you have to make a change. If you do what you have been doing, the way you've been doing it, you will get what you've been getting.

3) Not willing to let go.

St. John 5:6 says, *"When Jesus saw him lie, and knew he had been now a long time in that case, he saith unto him, Wilt thou me made whole?"* The scripture in this verse was specific in letting us know that Jesus knew the man had been there a long time. The bible does not tell us the man voluntarily told Jesus how long he had been in this situation. He just knew. Jesus also knows how long you've been going through, but he wants to know whether or not you are ready to be free. Are you really ready to let go? Wilt thou be made whole? Will you let him heal your hurts and scars? Will you let him pick up the pieces of your broken heart and put them back together again? Or will you continue to make excuses for not going forward. Will the pity party continue, or will you let Jesus do what he came there to do? Jesus was there to raise that man up, but it was up to him to allow Jesus to fulfill his purpose in him. Many times in the Gospels, Jesus would ask a question to whomever he was about to perform a miracle for. He wasn't just trying to get information, but a confession. He wanted to show them where they were in faith. When faith was manifested he had no reason for asking questions. He would make a statement such as, *"Thy faith has made thee whole."* In *St. Matthew 8:1-4*, there is a story of a man who was a leper. He came to Jesus with a whole different attitude than the man at the pool. He said to Christ in verse 2, *"Lord, if thou wilt, thou can make me clean."* Christ had no need to ask him, "Wilt thou be made whole?" The lepers faith was already at a level to receive his miracle. The point I'm trying to make is Jesus is always ready and willing to give, but are we ready to receive? Jesus said to the man with leprosy, *"I will: be thou clean, and immediately his leprosy was cleansed." St. Matthew 8:3.* Our freedom from grief and hurt can come much faster if we learn the art of casting. *"Casting all your cares upon him; for he careth for you." 1 Peter 5:7.* Once you cast your care in the right direction, you've got to implement the power of "let," which means allow. *"And let the peace of God rule in your heart, to which also ye are called in one body; and be thankful. Let the word of Christ dwell in you richly in all wisdom. Colossians 3:15-16.* This scripture came alive to me one day as I was visiting my son's grave alone for the first time. As I stood there I could feel the spirit of grief grasping at my soul until it took full possession of me. I ran to the car crying tears of despair and hopelessness. When I got to the car and sat down, I buried my face in my hands and continued to weep. Then this scripture came to me. It said, *"Let the peace of God rule your heart."* I realized it was up to me to either allow the peace of God to rule, or allow the spirit of grief to rule. I lifted my hand and prayed to God for his peace. At that very moment a peace, that is indescribable, entered into the car. I allowed God's peace to rule and was able to lift my head, dry my eyes, and drive from the cemetery with a whole new outlook. I remind you again, I'm not saying for you not to cry. I'm saying don't allow your grief to cause you to lose all hope. It's like the Apostle Paul told the church of the Thessalonians, *"But I would not have you to be ignorant, brethren, concerning them which are asleep, that ye sorrow not, even as others which have no hope." 1 Thessalonians 4:3.* He did not say not to have sorrow, for it would be impossible for us to lose someone we love dearly and not have sorrow. But we don't have to be sorrowful the same way others who have no hope. I can define negative grief as a grief that gives no hope toward inner healing of the body, soul, and spirit. The choice is up to you. Therefore, a change of attitude will inspire a change of altitude on our road to recovery.

4) Totally depending on man.

St. John 5:7 says, "The impotent man answered Him, Sir, I have no man, when the water is troubled, to put me into pool; but while I am coming, another steppeth down before me." Many times we trust in man to do only what God can do for us, and the things that God intends for man to do we want God to do. The impotent man must have spent many years waiting for someone to come along and help him win first place in the pool so he could be rewarded with complete healing in his body. Since nobody came to help him, he kept trying to do it on his own. The fact he said, "But while I am coming," lets us know that he was trying to make it on his own. This also tells us he must have had some ability to move on his own since he had no man there to assist him. How did he get there to begin with? I have found myself many times feeling hopeless and helpless because someone I trusted let me down. My expectations of friends were not met. Often, when we feel let down by one we trust, we purpose not to ever trust or depend on another. We often judge everybody by the actions of one or two. When we have only learned to depend on man and not God, and man fails, then our hope seems to dwindle down the drain. Man's extremity is God's opportunity, so we've heard it said. So, then ask yourself this, "Is God my first choice or is he my last resource?" There is nothing wrong with having a friend you can trust or believe in, but to become totally dependent on them is a dangerous place to be. I trust the opinion of my doctor. If I didn't, I wouldn't go to him. But when it comes to my total well-being, my hope, faith, and total trust are in the Lord. The same condition my doctor treats me for today, he may need treatment for himself tomorrow. It's like I said before, one can't pull me out of a pit he is in. *"For all have sinned, and come short of the glory of God." Romans 3:23.* Therefore we are in this together. We can help, comfort, encourage, and lift each other. But to pull us out, it takes something that goes beyond human intervention. It takes the power of a supreme being; it takes God. Many of us have been like the impotent man, trying to do it on our own, hoping someday we will get lucky. Well the word luck is not in God's vocabulary. He says, *"I call heaven and earth to record this day against you, that I have set before you life and death, blessing and cursing; therefore choose life, that both thou and thy seed may live." Deuteronomy 30:19.* You can change what you call luck into blessing by trusting totally in God and obeying him.

5) Unbelief and disobedience.

St. John 5:8 says "Jesus saith unto him, Rise, take up thy bed and walk." When Jesus said rise, take up thy bed and walk, all that was left for the impotent man to do was obey what Jesus told him to do. Jesus was telling him to do what he hadn't done in at least thirty-eight years. He could have complained and reminded Jesus that he was impotent and unable to walk. Instead, he trusted the power of Christ's words to him, *"Rise, take up they bed and walk."* These were not just words that sounded good. They were words that would change the course of this man's life, and could change the life of everyone who will obey. First we must be willing to rise. Raise our standard of living, raise our faith, and raise our attitude. Take the story of the prodigal son in *St. Luke 15*. It tells us of a young man who left home and spent all he had on riotous living. He ended up in the pig's pen, ready to eat what the pigs were eating. Then he came to his senses. The first thing he purposed in his heart to do was rise. Have you ever gotten down so low you found yourself ready to do something that was totally out of your character? Then you came to your senses and wondered, "What am I doing here?" You must rise up out of your pit.

Next Jesus said, *"Take up thy bed."* Why did he say this? He could have said, rise and walk. To take up thy bed means to remove the past. Leave nothing behind for you to go back to. You will never need the bed again so get it out of the way. Remember, he said take up thy bed, not make up thy bed. When you make up your bed, you're saying I am getting up from this place where I am, but I am making sure it is ready for me should I have to return. A made up bed is more inviting. Your bed could be your bad attitude, your short temper, jealousy or rebellion, the very things that support you while you are down. Jesus is saying take it up and get rid of it. Let inward healing begin.

After this Jesus said, *"Walk."* He wasn't asking the impotent man to demonstrate his newfound ability to walk. He was telling him to leave the place where he was. To walk means to move. To move means life. Even in the mother's womb the baby is expected to move. When we walk, we change. We are not stagnated by the same old thing. Doctors say that walking is one of the best exercises you can do for just about any condition. As you walk, you are strengthened. Each step gives you faith and courage to take another. When you reach the walking stage of your grief and loss, you are ready for restoration and recovery. You are a winner.

Apostle Eugene Satterwhite Th.D.

6) Traditions of men.

St. John 5:10 says *"The Jews therefore said unto him that was cured, it is the Sabbath day: it is not lawful for thee to carry thy bed."* What these self- righteous Jews didn't know is that under the law, there is death, but under grace, there is life. If you broke the law in the Old Testament it meant you died. Under the law the people were destroyed because of sin, but under grace, the sin is destroyed because of the people. *"...For this purpose was the Son of God manifested, that he might destroy the works of the devil."* When a denomination is more concerned about the keeping of their traditions than they are about the spiritual well-being of the people, then they are no different than these Jews who would rather see a man remain in a state of hopelessness than be free. Why were the Jews so concerned about this man now? Why did they not show concern when he was lying helpless by the pool? Where were they when he said, "I have no man?" It is amazing how some people never pay attention until you defy their beliefs. Any rule, belief, or law that does not contribute to the well-being of man is religious dogma and not real doctrine. The doctrine of Christ always brought life to the people and not limelight to the pulpit.

As I take another look at the man that had leprosy in *St. Matthew 8,* I realize that traditions and laws were broken here also. *"When he was come down from the mountain great multitudes followed him. And behold, there came a leper and worship him, saying Lord, if thou canst, make me clean. And Jesus put forth his hand and touched him, saying I will, be thou clean. And immediately his leprosy was cleansed." St. Matthew 8:1-3.*

First of all, the leper was not supposed to be in a public place where he could come in contact with other people. They were supposed to stay to themselves. Their only association was to be with other lepers. The leper really wanted a touch from God. He was willing to risk whatever it cost to seize the moment. He may never have gotten his chance again. What could they do to him that would make life any more miserable than what his life already was? In many cases death would be the best thing that could happen to a leper, especially if he is in his final stages. Like the four lepers outside the city in *2 Kings 7:3*. They said, *"Why sit here until we die?"* Their only hope was to trust what the man of God had said. If he was wrong, they would die. But no matter what else they did they were subject to death, so why not take this chance and believe what the man of God was asking. What did they have to lose?

Next let us look at what Jesus did. When Jesus saw the faith and persistence of this man to be healed, he must have thought within himself, "If he is willing to break laws and tradition and do what he's never done to get what he wants, then I will break laws and tradition to give him what he's never had." Jesus could have just spoken the word and the man would have been healed. Instead he broke the law by touching him. The law said if you touched a leper, you were considered unclean and were put out of the city for a certain period of time. Then you had to appear before the priest to see if you were still clean. Leprosy was a very contagious disease. What we must all remember is that what Jesus had was even more contagious. Therefore, instead of Jesus catching what the leper had the leper caught what Jesus had. Complete healing. Yes, just one touch from Jesus and you have whatever he has for you. He has deliverance and healing from depression, anger, bitterness, oppression, and negative grief. If you are willing to break the cycle that keeps you bound, then Jesus will meet you. To get what you never had you must be willing to do what you've never done.

Not all traditions are bad. I'm not in any way trying to encourage rebellion against the structure and standards set by the elders of an organization. I am saying every standard and bylaw should be Bible based in order to get Biblical results. In *St. John 5:16*, the scripture says they sought to kill Jesus just because he went against their doctrine. Anytime a denomination or religion seeks to destroy someone for doing well it is not Bible based.

Apostle Eugene Satterwhite Th.D.

7) Sin.

St. John 5:14 says *"Afterward Jesus findeth him in the temple, and said unto him, Behold, thou are made whole; sin no more, lest a worse thing come unto thee."* The fact that Jesus said, "Sin no more," is an indication sin may be why the person in the condition to begin with. When a person is battling with guilt of sin, it will cause hopelessness to grip his soul. You may start to feel like it is your sin that got you there and you can't do anything about it. You may start to feel like you deserve to have negative things happen to you. You can't see past your sin. You feel destined for failure. Remember, Jesus didn't say to this man what he said to most of the people he healed, *"Thy faith has made you whole."* He said, *"Behold thou art whole, sin no more lest a worse thing come unto thee."* In other words Jesus said, "it is not your faith that made you whole because you were depending on man, but it was your obedience and grace. You obeyed me in spite of what others thought, in spite of what tradition and laws. Therefore, my grace has restored thee." Sin no more so you won't have to deal with this, or something worse, again. Learn from your mistakes and you will grow spiritually.

No matter what the circumstances are surrounding your grief and loss, you should remember that past failure can either enhance or hinder future success depending on how well you learn and how willing you are to change.

When Mamas Go Home

It was a Tuesday, the 13th day of May, when I arrived at the hospital to see my mother. She was brought to the hospital about a week prior to this day with complaints of chest pain and difficulty breathing. It was her heart. She had minor surgery on her heart before; so many people didn't take her condition as seriously as it was. We later found out mother needed to have open-heart surgery. Although the doctors made no guarantees, we were assured her chances of complete recovery were good. Without the operation, mother could have a massive heart attack at anytime that could take her life. We told mother we would let her make her own decision concerning the operation. She agreed to have the operation. May 13 was the day the operation was to take place.

I was almost finished writing my second book entitled, "Good Grief For Hurting Hearts." I was scheduled to be on the Trinity Broadcasting Network that morning also. Mother's operation was at eight and the broadcast was at nine o'clock. I tried to convince my mother to let me cancel the television interview and be with her the whole time. She wouldn't hear of it. Since it was a five-hour operation and only a one-hour program, I had plenty of time to get back and be there before she got out of surgery.

When I arrived at the hospital it was about seven o'clock in the morning. All of the nurses greeted me like I was a celebrity. My mother told everyone about my television interview. She was so proud and excited. My mother had a way of making all eleven of her children feel like each of us was the best. The thought of my mother leaving me just never entered into my mind. Not one time did I allow myself to think, "What if she doesn't make it?" I just knew mother would be all right. My mother meant so much to me. I thought I could never live without her. Whenever she would talk to me about dying someday, I'd tell her, "Well, they'd better prepare to bury me also because I just couldn't take it." She was my mentor, my counselor and advisor, my hero, and my friend.

The television interview went well. I talked about grief. I gave my testimony of how God brought me through the death of our son. I told our viewers some of the things they could expect when the lose someone they love. It was nine o'clock in the morning. Little did I know that everything I said on television that morning would be staring me in the face that night. My mother died at about nine o'clock that night. I ran down the hospital hallway outside the intensive care unit, screaming. Again, I started feeling like God had let me down. I said to my wife, "I pray for those I love. When I am called on to pray for others, I seem to get answers, but when it's for me he doesn't answer." Words could not describe the pain I felt. If that old saying is true; "When you lose a parent, you lose a part of your past; when you lose a child you lose a part of your future." Right then I felt like I had lost my past and my future. All I had was now and my now didn't seem worth living. I went back into a deep depression. I didn't eat for the first two or three days after my mother's death. Normally, I would start overeating when I got depressed but I remembered my mother's words in one of our last conversations, "Eugene, you've got to get that weight off. Heart problems run in the family and that weight will make you more susceptible." So I purposed to eat very little or not at all.

The death of my mother made me discover something else. You can use grief from the death of one, to revive the grief of another who has died in the past. While mourning the loss of my mother, I would often take out a picture of my son and incorporate grief for him in with the loss of my mother. For a while I felt like I was losing control of my emotions. There were times I hurt so bad and wanted to cry but couldn't and other times I didn't want to cry but couldn't stop. I started to wonder, is this what it is like to have a nervous breakdown? How do I regain control of my life? What will I do without my mother? What will Thanksgiving and Christmas be like? She was our holiday. No matter how poor our family seemed to be, my mother always brought joy for the season. At Christmas, when she couldn't afford to buy the grandchildren gifts, mother would sew and make them pajamas and nightgowns. She was the best cook. No matter what she made, you could taste the love she put in it. How we miss her.

While I was putting myself through such torture by withdrawing and not eating, another dear mother at out church, Mother Willie Flemings, called me. She is also a loving sweet woman; I can truly call her mother. She didn't ask, but demanded I come over and see her. I got up with great curiosity and rushed over to see what was the urgent need for her to see me. When I got there I sat down and she came in. Her physical condition caused her to be nearly out of breath just walking from her bedroom to the living room. Mother Flemings heard about my negative behavior. She began to encourage me with rebuke. As tears welled up in her eyes, she said, "Sometimes when things like this happen, we think only of ourselves. We don't think about what might have been best for that person. When you get as old as your mom and me, there are times when we are in so much pain, sometimes you wish you could leave. Your mom and I had discussed the pain she faced and I am facing. There are times you just want to be free. You never know what she said to God, or what she was feeling. So you get up and go on with your life. Your mom is free from all pain. She'll never have to suffer again." Mother Fleming's gave me some money and made me promise to stop and eat some breakfast on my way home. I felt so much better.

After the mortician had prepared mother's body for viewing, I went to the funeral home and sat for hours. So many things came to my mind. I didn't understand why or how, but I was just waiting for mom to get up and talk to me one last time. As a matter of fact, I prayed for God to allow her to talk to me one more time. I knew that soon she would be put in the ground and I would never see this woman again. This is the woman that is responsible for my being here. She could have aborted me. She bore the pain for me to have life. She did for me what no one else could do. She loved me the way no one else could love me.

Needless to say, my mother never did get up and say anything to me, but as I was praying something happened. I remembered the last thing my mom and I did together was pray. I had held her hand and led us in prayer just before she went into surgery, and I went to the interview. As I sat in the funeral parlor praying, I heard a recording in my mind of one of the last conversations my mom and I had. I was about to move to Texas to help with a church and ministry founded by my spiritual mother. She was very ill and not expected to live much longer. I asked my mother, "Before I leave is there anything at all I can get you? Whatever you ask for, I'll try my best to get it. Anything at all." She said, "Eugene, you know there is really nothing I want that I don't have. I don't drive anymore so I don't need a car. I have clothes I have never worn. I'm having the time of my life. All I want is good health." At this point I heard a still small voice say, *"I have given her what you could not give her. Perfect health."* I then remember the words of Mother Flemings, she was right. Mom loved life and wanted to live but was tired of the pain and really wanted a change. I lifted my head and regained enough strength to get through the funeral. The minister's subject was, "She wanted to live, but she was ready to die." This is the poem I wrote for my mother's funeral as well as other poems dedicated to her:

I Saw Mama's Heart

I saw mama's heart last night,
And what a sight to behold,
It was strong and courageous,
A heart as pure as gold.

Though it had been weakened,
By the toils and snares of life,
It still held love for everyone,
Overflowing with love for Christ.

Her heart had a voice that always spoke,
Word to edify,
Her heart had ears that always hear,
Her children's painful cry.

Her heart had feet that traveled,
From near and from abroad,
Transporting prayers for those she loved,
That they would find peace with God.

Her heart had hands that always reached,
For a broken heart to mend,
To bring back joy and happiness,
And make them smile again.

Her heart had arms that comforted,
Those who were pushed aside,
All who sought its compassion,
They never were denied.

Then one day unexpectedly,
When her earthly task was complete,
God placed her heart in eternal care,
Where it will never cease to beat.

Apostle Eugene Satterwhite Th.D.

The memories of mama's heart,
Nothing or no one can ever erase,
Cause when Mama's heart stopped beating,
Or hearts picked up the pace.

Our Mother

For one of the world's greatest,
Words are hard to find,
To express our love in action,
We have to take the time.

To say how much we love you,
Words cannot tell it all,
Although others put us down,
With you we were ten feet tall.

Sometimes your children hurt you,
They caused you grief and pain,
But not once did you disown us,
Your love always remained.

I can't forget the yesterdays,
When ends just wouldn't meet,
When our fight seemed totally helpless,
You never did retreat.

As cook you are the greatest,
That's with everything you make,
The love you put in a pot of beans,
Couldn't taste better than steak.

You are also quite a seamstress,
That gift never went to waste,
The more we'd grow, the more you'd sew,
And still keep up the pace.

Most of us are grown now,
With children of our own,
And even your grandchildren,
Have experienced the love you have shown.

Apostle Eugene Satterwhite Th.D.

Your home is always open,
With warm and loving peace,
Somehow while in you presence,
Our bickering seems to cease.

You have fed, schooled, and clothed us,
You cooked and washed our dishes,
All you've done can't be repaid,
In word, deed, or riches.

There's so much more I could say,
But I don't want to bore you,
So all the things I cannot do,
I'll ask God to do for you.

"We Love You Mother Satterwhite"

From all Your Children

She's Gone To Be With Jesus

She's gone to be with Jesus,
Great victory to declare,
To leave life's toll and turmoil,
To rest in eternal care.

She's gone to be with Jesus,
To receive her crown well won,
She's gone to be with Jesus,
For her life has just begun.

She's no longer in this body,
Though fragments yet remain,
Great loss to me it seems to be,
Yet it's only heaven's gain.

On the day that mother left us,
Jesus stepped in the room,
With loving arm's reaching down,
To carry mother home.

She's gone to be with Jesus,
Where night is eternal day,
She's gone to be with Jesus,
Where tears are wiped away.

She's gone to be with Jesus,
Where soul is free from pain,
She's gone to be with Jesus,
Where death shall no longer reign.

So be encouraged loved ones,
To ever seek God's face,
For if you knew of the joy mother now has,
You'd long to take her place.

Apostle Eugene Satterwhite Th.D.

>But if we follow her example,
>To live life free from sin,
>And give heed to all her teaching,
>We'll see her face again.

A Change For The Better

The sunsets at evening tide,
Ushering in the night,
The morning dew is pushing through,
For soon the sun shines bright.

Bullfrog and butterflies,
Both experience change,
Behold the mountain glaciers,
That time doth rearrange.

Life is filled with changes,
In which we can't defy,
A time and season for all things,
A time to live and die.

I'm thinking of a precious friend,
How could I ever forget?
So much we could have said and done,
But time just wouldn't let.

She lived her life for Jesus,
Saved from worldly pleasure,
Her joy was in helping others,
There she found her treasure.

But now she too has seen a change,
A change that took her away,
To another home not made by hands,
From this earthly house of clay.

Now lift your head you loved ones,
Her soul is glory bound,
The trumpet shall sound, the dead shall rise,
No grave can keep her down.

Apostle Eugene Satterwhite Th.D.

We'll soon join her and the angels,
To sing through eternity,
When this corrupt puts on incorruptible,
And this mortal immortality.

We'll be caught up to meet the Lord,
Away in the middle of the air,
He'll take us to a prepared place,
There'll be no changes there.

Jesus Christ the same yesterday,
Today and forever more,
Shall be the light of the city,
No darkness shall endure.

Everyday is Sunday,
No pain, no death, no tears,
The flowers bloom forever,
We'll count no time by years.

So keep holding on to God's hand,
And wait till your change doth come,
Oh what joy will fill her soul,
To see us all come home.

Mother Won't Oversleep

I feel a feeling of emptiness,
A vacancy that cannot be filled,
That touch of love, the heavenly touch,
Through you God has revealed.

If I could turn back the clock,
To those precious moments shared,
I'd see your face lit with a smile,
And a heart that always cared.

I'd hear those words coming from your lips,
Of unpretending kindness,
A light that shines through thick and thin,
Through a world of sin and blindness.

I'd smell the beautiful fragrance you brought,
When the odors of sin abounds,
When others could only cry the blues,
You brought the joyful sounds.

Through the beauty of your life on earth,
An example for us is laid,
We now have precious memories,
Memories that will never fade.

You've slipped into that heavenly place,
You've finally made it home,
If we could bring you back again,
You wouldn't want to come.

Oh how much we'll miss you,
A million tears are shed,
But our greatest consolation,
Is in the words which Jesus said.

Apostle Eugene Satterwhite Th.D.

Let not your heart be troubled,
Only believe in me,
I'm going to prepare you a place.
Where you'll live eternally.

So take thy rest mother_____,
In God's tender loving care,
Wait for us in glory land,
For soon we'll all be there.

No place on earth can compare,
You're free from hurt and harm,
And you won't oversleep on that great day,
God's trumpet will be your alarm.

The trumpet shall sound, the dead shall rise,
And you'll be one of those,
Of whom the grave can't hold down,
You'll rise like Jesus rose.

I'll Be Waiting

My eyes have beheld the glory,
The beauty and joy of earth,
God's fabricated handiwork,
The mysteries of death and birth.

I've partaken of life's suffering,
I've felt the weight of the storm,
Waiting with great expectation,
For a better change to come.

And with no apparent warning,
In peace it silently came,
With a still small voice,
I hear him call my name.

Without delay or hesitation,
As the angels encouraged my reply,
I stepped out of this earthly house,
To a better home on high.

Death had no sting in that hour,
The account was settled before,
Death was merely a channel,
That led me to life evermore.

The announcement was made in heaven,
A new name for me was declared,
The welcome band was in order,
The great feast was prepared.

Heaven's choir started singing,
The music sounded so good,
Though I'll be missed by loved ones,
I wouldn't leave here if I could.

Apostle Eugene Satterwhite Th.D.

Set free from the toils of life,
No pressuring bills to pay,
God himself has taken my tears,
And eternally wiped them away.

No death, pain, or suffering,
No wounds to pacify,
Where peace flows like a river,
And nothing can ever die.

My feet walk on streets of gold,
There's emeralds, diamonds, and jade,
The water here is crystal clear,
And the flowers never fade.

The brightness of the city,
The natural eye can't bear,
There's not a shadow of darkness,
The Lambs light shines everywhere.

I just finished chatting with Moses,
I've visited Peter and John,
Paul and the other apostles,
Were so glad to see me come home.

There's not a dull moment in heaven,
The praises forever shall ring,
These few days I've been here,
I've been teaching the angel to sing.

So don't worry about me dear ones,
Do all for God you can do,
Totally commit your life to him,
And I'll be waiting in heaven for you.

Good Grief for Hurting Hearts

Mommy

They say she's gone, I say they're wrong,
Oh, How could it be?
She prayed, she cried, she lived, and she died,
From earthly realm set free.

Where are those sparkling eyes of hope?
Those ears that heard our cry,
The gentle touch, we loved so much,
The memory will never die.

Where is the heart of love and desire?
To help her fellow man,
The one on the street, with no food to eat,
Where is that helping hand?

They say she's gone, I say they're wrong,
Oh, How could it be?
She was cried on, then lied on, yet she did fight on,
In God she found her victory.

Where is that loving motherly smile?
Brightening days full of gloom,
All who knew of her, couldn't help but love her,
For hate her heart held no room.

Where are those feet that would walk a mile?
With no selfish motive in mind,
She was ears for some, a tongue for the dumb,
She gave here eyes for the blind.

Where is mommy? Oh can't you see,
Where the soul is always well,
Lying there, Oh that's not her,
It's just an empty shell.

Apostle Eugene Satterwhite Th.D.

Her eyes see no more evil,
Her feet walk on streets of gold,
Her ears hear heavenly music,
Her heart will never grow cold.

Her smile is seen by angels,
She's touched the Master's hand,
She's given us a great example,
Fulfilling life's demand.

They say she's gone, I say they're wrong,
Now you may ask me why,
They say she's gone, I say they're wrong,
She lives on in you and I.

Mother, We're On Our Way

There is now a sweet voice missing,
During our time of family prayer,
Our hearts are already longing,
For her smiles to be there.

But we've not really lost her,
She has only moved away,
To a better home in glory,
From that earthly house of clay.

She will always be remembered,
Her love will never depart,
The seed of her great teaching,
Remains within our heart.

She was a dedicated Christian,
With a walk so pure and clean,
She held up the blood stained banner,
God's love was always seen.

She walked so close to Jesus,
Her prayers were always heard,
She led us in His footsteps,
She taught us through His word.

Oh, how we love you mother,
Sleep on, take thy rest,
Cause on resurrection morning,
You'll rise up and be blessed.

And we that are alive and remain,
Shall soon be caught up too,
As Jesus comes with angels,
We'll again join hands with you.

Apostle Eugene Satterwhite Th.D.

By following your great teaching,
Well done, We'll hear him say,
We'll all be home at supper time,
Mother, we are on our way.

About six months after the death of my mother, within the same year, tragedy struck again. My spiritual mother Dr. Theresa Martin died. Thirty years ago her powerful preaching and teaching of the gospel pricked my heart and caused me to change my life. Since then she had been one of my major sources of strength and encouragement. She had always been there for me. She is the main reason why I moved to Texas. Mother Martin had been sick for a long time, but she never really made it known to everyone. Very few people really knew how sick she was. About a year before her death, my spiritual mother talked to me about her ministry in Texas and what would become of it when she died. She expressed a desire for me to take over the work.

At that time things were seemingly going great for me in Tacoma. I thought within myself there is no way I would move to Texas. At that time I was having blueprints drawn to build a new home in Tacoma. My wife was providing care for her sick father, who was living with us at the time. Since he was a veteran, she was scheduled to receive top pay for providing in home care for him. In the process, we discovered he had a G.I. bill he never used and we were approved to have our home built without a down payment as long as he signed on the deed. With the money we would have used for a down payment we decided to open a small fast food restaurant next to my son's barbershop. There was a wealthy businessman who had agreed to help us with the remodeling expense. Everything looked perfect, so Texas was out. Within just a few short months after that conversation with Mother Martin, everything seemed to have changed for me. My father-in-law died. It was also before he signed the G.I. bill for the house. They mailed the approval out but we didn't get it in the mail until after his funeral. By now, we had spent our down payment to build our home. The shrewd businessman that had agreed to help us rescinded at the last moment for no apparent reason. He made us do a song and dance and meet all his foolish demands, then simply told us he couldn't or wouldn't help us. My wife and I were devastated as we again watched our dreams go up in smoke. Her father's death was painful enough without all the other losses we had to face. After evaluating everything that had happened, I was ready for a change. I felt this was God's way of letting me know I was supposed to be in Texas. Every door had closed for me in Washington, so we made the decision to move to Texas.

Prior to moving to Texas, I visited the church there for a business meeting in which Mother Martin announced I would be moving to Texas to pastor the church. Everyone seemed so excited. She gave members a chance to express themselves. They made me feel like the six million dollar man. No one had anything negative to say. My dreams seemed to have been resurrected. It was a small group but we were all like family. I was ready to put my vision into action.

There were about eight families that moved to Texas with me. Almost immediately the two congregations clashed. Nothing seemed to be going right. There were problems and confrontation from the very start. I'm not going to belittle my integrity by pointing the finger at one group or the other. All I can say is it didn't work out and I felt I had to resign after only being there a few months. The pain I felt from the whole ordeal had to be worse than having a knife put in my chest. My heart felt like a punching bag and those I dearly loved, seemed to be taking turns striking it. No one on earth can hurt you like a person who calls you brother. I started to believe there was something really wrong with me and asked, "Why am I being treated like the bad guy?" I love people. I left a church full of people that really loved me to come to Texas to be rejected. I had to turn it over to God and let him sort it all out. It was too much for me.

After nearly twenty years of pastoring, here I was having to start all over again. The odds seemed to be against me. I only had eight families; I had no church building, equipment, and no money. I was in a city I knew nothing about. I felt lost and without hope. It was God and the faithful few that helped me regain faith in myself, and the ministry he had given me. I was again ready for war. The hardest thing was letting go of what might have been.

Apostle Eugene Satterwhite Th.D.

Heaven In My View

One of the greatest experiences I have ever had was when I was visited by an angel who took me to heaven to tour my mansion. This experience has made it easier for me to live with losing someone I love, especially if they were born again believers. I was preaching a revival in Ft. Worth, Texas. I was living in Washington state at this time. The revival turned out to be a success. One night during the revival, the spirit of God came in the service in a powerful, yet unusual manner. I prayed and sang prophecy to nearly everyone in the building. Afterwards, Mother Theresa Martin prayed for me. The prayer was so powerful, it seemed to take me to another realm.

When the service ended, mother and I were sitting upstairs in the apartment dining area that was connected to the church. All of a sudden, I looked in the doorway and there was an angel. Though the whole area was completely lit from the glory of this heavenly being, no one saw it but me. Tears were streaming down my face as I tried to explain to Mother what I was seeing. I stood and began reaching for him. In what seemed to be the blink of an eye, he took off straight through the ceiling. Somehow, I managed to grab hold of his garment as he left. This all happened so fast it was hard to explain. I was caught somewhere between mortality and immortality. In a matter of seconds, I was with the angel before his beautiful gate. The gate opened and the angel made his entrance so quickly he shook off my grip and left me outside as the door quickly closed.

I got a brief glimpse of that city. The glory that exhilarated from the city was more than the natural eye could behold. The peace I felt from those few seconds of exposure to heaven's bliss was like none I had ever known. Then, I heard the voice of Mother Martin calling my name. She knew what was happening. I was so engrossed by heaven's splendor I had no thoughts of returning to this earthly life. The experience let me know loved ones who have gone on to be with the Lord wouldn't come back here if they could. When I finally came to, I could hear mother saying, "Come back, come back, you can't go yet. It is not your time. God has a great work for you to do. Come back." When I sat down in the seat, my whole body felt numb. Have you ever had your hand or other parts of your body fall asleep? Well that's how I felt all over.

I looked at Mother Martin with great anger in my eyes and said, "Why did you pray me back? Why would God allow me to see the glory and experience such unspeakable joy and bring me back here?" She said, "Because your work is not finished. You can't go now. You had this experience to help keep you on the right track no matter what comes your way." I got up and went to bed. My heart was very heavy. Even though I had a beautiful wife, three fine sons, and a host of family and friends, I was ready to leave it all for what I saw that night. Although that night was quite traumatic, the real highlight of the story took place the following morning. I was sitting on the bed reminiscing about the night before, when there appeared before me another angel. He was dressed in a long white gown and looked like a normal man with a glow luminating from him. I noticed his feet were not touching the floor. I was not hallucinating or dreaming. I was wide-awake and in my right mind. I have had visitations from angels before but this was quite different. I've had angels come to me when everyone that was with me saw them too. Normally, I would get so excited I could hardly keep my composure but I guess the Lord gave me the previous night's experience to prepare me for the next day. The angel reached out his hand for me to come.

I calmly stretched my hand toward him. He grabbed my hand and lifted me from the bed. I started walking with him through mid air. The most awesome thing I had ever felt or witnessed was when I looked back and saw my body still lying motionless on the bed. I heard of people having out of body experiences, but I never dreamed it would be like this. I remember just after leaving the room there was a dark tunnel. The next thing I knew I was standing in front of the most beautiful mansion. It was indescribable. I have a better understanding of the term, 'beauty beyond compare.' There is nothing on earth I could compare to what I saw. It's like seeing a color you are unfamiliar with. I know what I saw, but it's hard to put into words so the natural mind can understand. I saw seven angels harboring around the mansion and two at the front door. The angel said to me, "These represent the Fruit of the Spirit. Because these fruit were manifested in your life on earth, these angels are here to serve you through eternity." There was so much knowledge I gained from this experience; that's what made the experience so real. I've never been able to buy a lot of expensive diamonds or gold, but at the mansion there were diamond laced walkways and the street that ran in front was paved with gold. The angel then said, "Gold is one of earth's most valued resources so they use cheap stuff like rock and tar to make their streets. But gold is so cheap in heaven that the streets are paved with it." Another thing I noticed was there were no lights in the city, the way I know light. Yet there wasn't even a shadow of darkness. The brightness of the city came from the throne. As we walked toward the mansion, I saw it was surrounded by the most beautiful floral arrangement ever witnessed by man. I've seen the big flower parades that exploit all the colorful flowers. I've visited flower gardens that are said to be the greatest. But none could compare to the excellent glory radiating from these flowers. There were flowers of every kind. Some I'd never seen before. The angel then said to me, "These flowers bloom all year round. They are flawless and they never die. On earth, to judge if a plant is real or artificial, you look for signs of death." What a revelation I received from this. My wife and I love flowers and plants and sometimes we would go out to different places and see plants and wonder whether they were real or artificial. After this lesson from the angel, I never wondered again. I also incorporated this message with my preaching, "If a person is a real true Christian then there should be signs of death. For the Bible lets us know we are dead to sin."

Good Grief for Hurting Hearts

When we got inside the mansion I was again in amazement, because nothing I saw could be related to what I know now about what a home should look like. I do remember seeing these huge posts and on one of them there was a name written that puzzled me for months later. It read, Eloiumnium. I searched through dictionaries and other word translation books and could not yet get a full understanding of this name. Maybe it's my new name that's written down in glory.

The angel started to take me down what appeared to be a hallway, then he paused and turned and said, "We can't go that way yet, it's not finished." I thought, why am I here in an unfinished mansion? But I never asked him. Next he took me to an area that looked like it could have been a kitchen but there was no food there. When I asked about the food, he led me to the back of the mansion. The entire back yard was a garden. Everything was in a state of ultimate perfection. Every fruit and vegetable held its natural color. This had to be what the Garden of Eden was like before Adam sinned. God's presence seemed to fill every crevice in the garden. I looked and saw a river flowing through the middle of the garden. It was the water that looked like freshly polished crystal. It was so clear and pure you could taste it with your eyes. Then all of a sudden I heard a loud sound of praises and admiration that seemed to be coming from the front of the mansion. The sound was so loud and startling I didn't wait for my guide. I ran around to the front to see what all the commotion was. As I looked down the streets of gold, I saw coming toward the mansion, a luminated figure of a man dressed in a long gown. I've never seen a million of anything before but I knew there must have been a million little angels flying around worshipping this heavenly being. They were saying, "Holy, Holy, Holy is the Lamb, slain from the foundation of the world." I knew right away it was Jesus.

As he came closer, I could see he was carrying a golden crown decorated with stars that seemed so bright. Uncontrollable tears flowed from my eyes as I fell to my knees. I thought within myself how unworthy I was to receive anything

Apostle Eugene Satterwhite Th.D.

at all from Jesus. I felt like all he's ever done was give. He gave his life for me, he gave me life, and he blessed me with so much in life for so long, now I felt like I should be giving him something. But what could I give him? While I was kneeling with my head hung down I felt his presence overshadow me. My heart seemed paralyzed with reverent fear. I took courage and began to raise my head anticipating looking into those loving eyes. As I raised my head, he lowered the crown. The split second the crown touched my head I felt my spirit leap back into my body and I jumped straight up in my bed. Again, my whole body felt numb. I knew I had been in the presence of the almighty God. I spent the next three days crying. Every time I'd think about what happened I'd start crying. This experience came years before my son or my mother died. I know they are really in a better place and one day I'll join them and we'll be together forever.

I Have A Dream, But It's A Set Up

If you read the book of Genesis, chapters 37-50, you will find the story of Joseph. Joseph was a dreamer and interpreter of dreams. His life took him down a road I'll call 4 P's road: the pit, Potiphar's house, prison, and the palace. In his dream Joseph only saw the palace. He did not see the road he would have to take to get there. How many times in a good church service have you had an evangelist or prophet tell you of God's blessings on your life? You stand in the prayer line expecting to hear a good word from the Lord.

Generally, they only tell you about your palace. They tell you how you are about to be blessed, that material wealth is coming your way, and God is going to grant your heart's desire. They generally don't tell you about the pit, Potiphar's house, or the prison. Therefore, many die spiritually before they reach their palace. When you get a good word promise, start preparing for the pit instead of expecting the palace the next day. There has got to be a change of attitude. Jesus said, *"He that is faithful over a few things I will make him ruler over many."* Many people want to be rulers without being faithful. The things Joseph suffered on his road to the palace prepared him for leadership in the palace. The direction of his life seemed to be totally opposite of what he saw in his dream. When he was going through his hardships he had to hold on to his dream. All we have to hold on to sometimes is a dream or vision that God has given us.

The Pit

The pit is a place in our life where we recognize our need for God. It is the place where you find salvation. It is where you are dependent on a higher source to lift you out. If you are not taken out of the pit, you will face certain death. Joseph was taken from the pit and sold like property. As Christians, we too have been bought with a price. The bible says in *1 Corinthians 6:20, "For ye are bought with a price: therefore glorify God in your body, and in your spirit, which are God's."* In the pit you realize you are helpless without God. You are lost. The worst person in the world is a person who is lost and doesn't know it. If you don't know you are lost, you will keep traveling the road you are on until you reach an unexpected destination. David says in *Psalms 40:1-2, "I waited patiently for the Lord, and he inclined unto me and heard my cry. He brought me up also out of a horrible pit, out of the miry clay, and set my feet upon a rock and established my goings."*

We must remember that Joseph did nothing wrong to be put in the pit. He just shared his dream with those he thought really cared. The worst pain one can experience is pain caused by those who say they love you. No one can hurt you like your brethren. No wonder David said in *Psalms 55:12-13, "For it was not an enemy that reproached me; then I could have borne it: neither was it he that hated me that did magnify himself against me; then I would have hid myself from him: But it was thou, a man mine equal, my guide, mine acquaintance."*

Potiphar's House

Potiphar's house is a place where you learn to be a servant. *St. Mark 10:44* reads, *"And whosoever of you will be the chiefs, shall be servant of all."* Once you've come out of the pit you must learn to serve. Joseph could have gone to Potiphar's house with a negative attitude. He could have held bitterness and animosity against his brethren who caused him to be there. His ill feelings would have affected his ability to serve. Instead he did not let his negative past dictate his future. He gave the best of his service in spite of the pain caused by those he loved. Your emotions will determine how well you serve. If you are angry, it shows in everything you do. Joseph chose to forgive; he chose not to let the actions of others dictate his future.

The next thing you have to do at Potiphar's house is pass the integrity test. Joseph was tempted by Potiphar's wife. He could have easily yielded but he chose to maintain his integrity. I always thought we were supposed to resist temptation, but we are not. We are to flee! Joseph fled. How could a man stand over a naked woman and resist? He must flee. Joseph passed his integrity test. He was ready to move closer to the palace. Often when we face life's traumas, things seem to go from bad to worse. Our dreams and desires seem to be moving farther and farther from reality. Remember, it's only a set up to keep you from getting to the palace.

Prison

Prison is a place where you learn total submission. You are totally committed to the will of those in authority. You cannot even wear what you want. You are told when to eat, sleep, work, and play. You no longer control your own life. *Romans 12:1* says, *"I beseech you, therefore brethren, by the mercies of God, that ye present your bodies a living sacrifice, holy, acceptable unto God, which is your reasonable service."* Joseph could have again held anger and bitterness in his heart because he was falsely accused. No doubt thoughts must have entered his mind, such as, "How can I ever get to the palace being a convicted felon? I will never see my dreams fulfilled now. I am just hoping against hope." Instead of entertaining those negative thoughts, Joseph continued to serve. In prison he gave himself to help others. When two of his fellow inmates had a dream, he was more than willing to give the interpretation of the dream. This act ultimately lead him to his destiny.

Your spiritual prison may be financial or physical bondage. It could be any number of things that keep you from seeing your dreams fulfilled. Many times, like Jesus, you must look in the cup. He must have seen the cross and suffering and he prayed, *"If it be possible let this cup pass."* I believe Jesus took another look and saw the salvation of mankind and prayed, *"Thy will be done."* Sometimes when it seems you're farthest from your palace, you are closest to it.

The Palace

The palace is the place of maturity. It is where your dreams are fulfilled. Your needs are met and you still know how to serve and submit. In the palace you can see a better picture of why you had to take the road you took. Like Shadrach, Meshach, and Abednego, you had to stay in the fire long enough for your enemy to recognize God is walking with you. Like David, you have to learn from the lion and bear experience, and are now ready to fight for the lives of your brethren and go against the giant. When David killed the lion and the bear, that was his personal battle. When he went against the giant, he was in warfare for the brethren. Don't ever try to conquer the giant in your life before you learn how to conquer the lion and bear. You can't help your brethren until you can help yourself. Spiritual warfare begins with conquering your flesh and its evil desires. When Joseph reached the palace he was put in a place where he could save his family and preserve the nation of Israel. God had set him up; therefore his suffering was not about him, but about the salvation of a nation. Could you imagine what would have happened if Joseph would have given up on life while he was in the pit, escaped from Potiphar's house, or committed suicide in prison? God would have had to seek another person to fulfill his plan, and Joseph would have missed his palace.

It's Not Over Till It's Over

Many people have asked me, do I really get over the loss of a loved one? It depends on the individual and how they define 'getting over.' To some 'getting over' means forgetting and never feeling the pain. If that were the case then I will never get over the loss of my son and my mother. 'Getting over' means to learn to accept the loss and live with it without depression, resentment, anger, or bitterness. Sometimes you have to get over these hurdles one at a time. Time has a way of healing past hurts and losses. I will never get over the fact my son is dead. His death is something I will have to face the rest of my life. I can't change that but I can change the way I deal with it. What we really need to get over is not so much the death of a loved one, but the negative methods we use to deal with the loss.

Though years have passed since the death of my son, I can't truly say I have gotten over it. There are constant reminders that trigger things about him. Every time I see a basketball game I think of Jerome. He loved basketball. A picture, a piece of clothing, or just certain sceneries may trigger my grief but it doesn't have to be negative grief. To be truthful, I'm not trying to get over the loss of those I love; I just strive daily to deal better with it. I want to remember the good times we shared. Precious memories are the most valuable thing I have left of my loved ones. Precious memories!

I have certain video recordings of my mother that trigger grief every time I watch them. There are certain times of the year that automatically bring bittersweet memories of events we shared together or something tragic took place. It's funny how grief has a way of reminding us of certain things. I used to always forget my son's birthday, but since he's been gone, I've never forgotten the day he died. Even when I'm out ministering in another city, the day of his death comes to my mind. There were times when I have felt a certain sadness come on and not know why, then my wife will bring to my attention that it is Jerome's birthday or close to the day he died.

I found one of the hardest things to get over after the death of a loved one is the realization of major events you will have to spend without them. For instance, the first Christmas without mother created an irreplaceable void. No holiday will ever be the same. I developed a literal fear of May coming around. May brought a threefold trauma for me. It was my mother's birthday, Mothers Day, and she died in May. May is supposed to be the most beautiful time of the year. The spring flowers are blossoming as temperatures began to heat up in preparation for summer. The question haunted my mind, with all the beauty and splendor of May, would I ever smile and enjoy it again? I had to come to grips with myself and say, "It's not over till it's over." I had to realize if I allowed myself to let negative grief rob me of the splendor of spring, it would soon claim my summer sun, then my awesome autumns and my fabulous falls.

You see I can think of something negative that has happened to me each month of the year. I can't afford to let these things control my life and dictate to me my level of happiness. I had to find a way to combat the fear of facing certain days. The best way to fight negative grief is to replace it with positive thought patterns. I had to view life as the four seasons of the year. Each season brings about a change must adapt. Rain, snow, and cold weather may inconvenience us but they play a great part in the earth's survival. We don't give up on life because it rains or snows; we know the season will change. We must learn to make adjustments for the storms we face in life.

I took back my life when I began to think about all the reasons I had to be happy instead of depressed at certain times of the year, even in the spring and the month of May. I remember too, it was the spring when my youngest son was born. On my mother's birthday in May our first granddaughter was born. It was May I graduated from Bible College with a TH.D. It was in May the church I have pastored for nearly twenty years was born. I could go on and on but I think you get the picture. The experience I gained the first May I faced after my mother's death has caused me to look forward to the next. I can face it with a new graciousness and a positive outlook. I don't know when the rain may fall on my May again, but it could never dim the sunlight that has already shined forth its light.

I am learning day-by-day and step-by-step how to turn negative grief into a positive tool that will assist others in overcoming the process. Anything in life gets easier when you learn to deal with it. The hurt and pain may be the same as always but it seems easier as we learn how to adjust. A one hundred and fifty pound barbell may seem heavy to a man who is just beginning weightlifting. After several moths of lifting, the barbell will seem lighter. When carrying the weight of grief, you've got to know what to hold on to and what to let go. You cannot carry the total weight all the time. If I have learned anything as a pastor, I've learned in dealing with people I've got to be careful not to try to carry all their burdens and not my own. I listen to problems sometimes all day long. If I'm not careful, I will find myself down and out over what is really not my problem. I can't pull anyone from a pit if I decide to jump in there with them. If I do jump in with them I had better make sure I have something strong enough to support us both in getting out. I have learned to cast it over on the Lord. Since Christ already died for the sins of the world, I don't have to kill myself trying to fix everyone's problems. I realized when I am dead and gone people will still have problems but only one less person to tell them to. I've determined I must let God do what he does best, take control.

Getting over the negative way we deal with loss can be difficult when there are things that constantly remind you of what you are missing. I believe everyone wants to be remembered when they are gone. Jesus told us to take communion in remembrance of Him. He wanted to be remembered. Certain things may occur that will make you wonder if the deceased one is trying in some way to make us remember. I remember at one of our family reunions something happened that made us all wonder. Each year we would have T-shirts made with all the names of immediate family members and their children. When the shirts were run on the press, Jerome's name came out in a bigger, bolder print than the other names on the shirt. His name was printed the same on the master copy but when printed on the shirt, it seemed to stand out above the others. It was almost like he was saying, "Remember me, while you are all fellowshipping and enjoying each other." That family reunion in my opinion turned out to be the best one we ever had or have had since. It was at this reunion we recorded the best video of our mother. She gave a speech at the end of the video as if she knew she wouldn't be with us much longer. She spoke about how she was glad to live near her grandchildren and even some great-grandchildren. She shared her appreciation for her children and encouraged us to keep going. The tape has become my most valued possession.

To bring to finality the negative grief in your life, there are certain principles that must be applied. Here are five basic principles: (1) communication, (2) keeping a positive attitude, (3) use opposition as a good character building tool, (4) take time to minister to yourself, and (5) take care of your physical body with proper diet and exercise.

1) Communication.

When you feel like you are going to explode with grief, open your mouth and express your feelings to someone. Keeping things bottled up inside will only prolong the grief process, and it could even make you ill. Support groups are sometime good to attend. People who have been through similar traumas can freely communicate their feelings to others without fear of rebuttal. Sometimes it helps to know you are not the only one going through this pain. Sometimes it helps to loosen the fountain of tears you've held bottled up inside you when you begin to open up and talk about the loss. Something someone else says may trigger some emotions that will help you vent.

There are times when you feel alone and you don't have anyone to talk to, well try prayer. Talking to God is the most therapeutic method of recovery I know. He truly knows and cares about your pain. He always has time to listen. *I Peter 5:7* says, *"Casting all your cares upon him, for he careth for you."* Many times when I felt like the weight of the world was on my shoulders, I found sweet relief in prayer. I felt so much lighter after talking to God. Prayer doesn't always change situtations, but it will change you and help you accept things that were not meant to be.

2) Keeping A Positive Attitude.

As long as you are dwelling on negative thoughts it will be hard for you to develop a positive attitude. Many times when I feel down and like all is against me, I start counting my blessings. They always seem to outnumber my problems. I remember recently complaining to myself about all the bad things that had happened to me in my life. All of a sudden that still small voice from within me said, "You have more to be thankful for than you have to be angry about. You have never spent one night under the bridge because of homelessness. You have never had to dig through garbage cans to find your daily meal. You got up out of bed on your own and went to the bathroom on your own. As a grown man no one has ever had to change your diaper for you or bathe you. You have all the activities of your limbs. You should be grateful because no matter how bad your condition is, there is someone who would love to be in your shoes." I had to learn how to change my emotions of anger and resentment to joy and gratefulness. I had to start to focus on what I have and not what I lost. I had to start appreciating life and accepting grief and loss as an inevitable part of it. I believe the success or failure in one's struggle to overcome is based on the individual's attitude. It alone can change your destiny. The toll the storms of life take on our physical and spiritual man will be determined by our attitude.

3) Use Opposition As A Good Character Building Tool.

The most powerful witness that has been manifested in my life was my overcoming hardship and pain. There had been people who were professing to be atheists come to me after seeing me endure grief and loss and say they know now there is something to what I believe. They recognized I have something they don't and they could never endure such pain and maintain their faith. It was not my preaching or witnessing to them that got their attention. It was their seeing how I was able to endure opposition.

When life throws hard stones your way you can do one of several things. You can let them bury you, you can let them cause you continual pain, you can build a wall and isolate yourself behind them, or you can use them as stepping stones to take you to higher ground. If you use them as an elevation tool, you will find you can look down on your problems and get a clearer overall view of what is happening. You will be able to clear your mind. You will view life as a complete challenge. You will no longer feel like a victim of misfortune who has been predestined for failure. With every victory you gain strength to overcome the next challenge. Opposition should be viewed as an opportunity to exercise faith. The more faith is exercised, the stronger faith will become. The stronger your faith, the better will be your character.

4) Take Time To Minister To You.

There is a saying, "An idle mind is the devil's workshop." I agree. I believe bad habits or addictions when they are broken must be replaced by something. We will either develop more negative habits or more positive ones. It's like the drug addict that went from heroin to cocaine. Many people I know who used to be heavy smokers are now heavy overeaters. I heard a story of a man that was so heavy he was confined to his bed. He didn't have a life. He couldn't do anything for himself but eat. Food became his narcotic to help him deal with life's issues. The thing that caused the problem has now become the problem. In other words, he started eating because he was depressed, now he's depressed because he can't stop eating.

In order to deal better with my loss, I had to fill my life with things I enjoyed doing. Too much free time was not good for me. I had to take time to minister to my own needs. Since I loved water and swimming, I decided to take up scuba diving. It was very good therapy. I found such peace. It was like entering another world. Scuba diving was a way of escape for me. I would suggest to everyone who has to deal with grief and loss, to find themselves an outlet. If you don't have a hobby, find one. Start volunteering to do social work, helping others deal with what you have gone through. By helping others, remember, you are also helping yourself.

5) Take Care Of Your Physical Body With Proper Diet And Exercise.

Staying physically fit will also help enhance the healing process of grief and loss. The way I feel physically will affect the way I react spiritually. Being physically fit gives me one less reason to be depressed. I can at least feel good about myself, even if I don't feel good about what's happening around me. Proper diet and exercise work together. I found when I am on a regular exercise program it is easier for me to eat a proper diet. If I exercise and then overeat, I feel my workout is in vain. I'm able to refrain from certain fatty foods. It's funny how the body never seems to crave the things that are good for us. I've never felt an irresistible urge for a piece of broccoli, parsley, carrots, or onions, which are the highest in nutrients. Medical science has discovered we do crave these things but they are not appeasing to our sensual taste buds. We don't really know our bodies. We don't understand what our body is really craving. The test is in how our bodies respond. The body responds best to those true cravings. Our bodies crave nutrients and minerals that are necessary for survival. What feels and tastes good is not always good. We have acquired cravings and not instinctive cravings. If we never used salt, food would taste fine without it. You must find out whether you are eating to fulfill a need or a lust for certain types of food.

If you're eating to fulfill a lust, then you will have to eat more. Lust is never satisfied. The more you eat, the more you want. You may get a one-time fulfillment but it's coming up again. When things are going wrong a person feels like they are losing control. They may feel like there is nothing they can do to change their condition. They therefore do the thing that feels good to them, they eat. I've talked to overweight people who tell me the only thing they can do to make them feel better about their condition was to eat. Those that over eat as an excuse to cover up pain always seem to eat the wrong things. Too much of anything is not good for you. Even too much exercise can be a hazard to your health. Your body is designed for rest. One of the basic needs for man is rest. Some of the best rest the body can get is rest from eating. Fasting is the fastest way to lose weight physically, gain strength spiritually, and get refreshed mentally. Many animals express their grief and loss by fasting. Some doctors suggest everyone should fast at least one day a week and ten full days once a year. This will clean all the poison and harmful toxins out of your system from the food we eat. I have never felt better in all my life than after a long fast. My complexion is clear from all blemishes, my teeth are whiter, I feel more energetic, and I can think a lot clearer. Those are just a few of the benefits of fasting, not to mention the spiritual growth one can experience. It will help open your eyes to the truth so you can better cope with whatever life offers you.

Breaking The Cycle

The word cycle is defined as a period of time within which a round of regular recurring events are completed. Our grief cycle can take us in circles. We will often find ourselves worn out, but not really getting anything accomplished. We find ourselves constantly moving but not going anywhere. Just when we get over one hurdle another one sticks up its head. The cycle must be broken for us to experience change. Whether your cycle is grief and loss, financial, mental, or physical, there are positive ways to break the cycle. Here are four ways to break the negative cycle:

1) Stop It.

When a car, vacuum cleaner, washing machine, or any other appliance stops functioning properly the first thing we do is stop it. You don't try to fix a car when it is still running. Many times we end up in a cycle because we don't stop long enough to find out what is going on. Our Christian faith teaches us to keep going, hold on, and don't give up no matter what. We should also know that sometimes we need to stop and take inventory. When you're carrying a heavy load and you feel like you could lose it, then sometimes you must let go, set the load down, and get a fresh grip. If not, you may cause injury to yourself and those who are helping you. Stopping doesn't mean quitting. It means taking the time to acknowledge the problem and construct a method to resolve it.

2) Study It.

David said in *Psalms 119:59 "I thought on my ways and turned my feet unto thy testimonies."* Grief and loss has taught me so much about myself. There were things I would have never found out had it not been for my experiences with grief and loss. Before one can be a good mechanic and fix the car's problem, that person must study to see what makes the car run properly. Since people are different in many ways, we must learn about ourselves and know what it takes to get us functioning properly. Although there are those that will help counsel and encourage me, I am still the chief mechanic in the rebuilding of my broken life. No goals can be achieved without my assistance. I must study myself. What makes me do what I do? In studying myself I found there were things I hated about myself that I needed to change in order for me to be happy with me. As a Christian, my ultimate goal is to be Christ-like. I had to begin to eliminate from my life all the things that were not Christ like. I now have a purpose and an achievable goal. I have a perfect example to follow. The bible says in *1 Peter 2:21-23 "For even hereunto were ye called, because Christ also suffered for us, leaving us an example, that ye should follow in his steps; who did no sin, neither was guile found in His mouth; who, when he was reviled, reviled not again; when he suffered, he threatened not but committed himself to him that judgeth righteously."*

3) Fix It.

Many times the cost is too high to fix something. If it is still running, we will continue to use it until it breaks down completely. Remember you will either pay now or later. When the brakes on your car start to squeak, that's the time you need to fix them. It is better to buy brake shoes or pads now than to have to buy the whole rotor later. In other words, it's better to deal with anger now than rage later or pornography now than adultery later. Don't let negative traits linger without dealing with them. They won't just go away or get better. You have to work on fixing these traits. You can either cure the cause or treat the symptoms. A car may run hot because it's low on water but if it continues to run hot there is something more serious that needs to be considered. I have seen cars run for months with a leaky hose, a bad water pump, or a thermostat. The owner didn't want to fix the problem so he just kept adding water each time the water level ran low. In doing so, the owner was taking the risk of having the motor overheat and be ruined forever.

The word of God is a powerful tool for fixing the broken parts of our lives. It can serve as a wrench to tighten up the loose ends, just as a screwdriver to give us a solid grip on a firm foundation and as a visegrip to hold it in place when things get a little shaky. Sometimes it is not good to try to fix things on your own, especially if you've never had to deal with it before. You sometimes need the assistance of a more experienced mechanic to help you find and fix the problem.

4) Redirect It.

2 Chronicles 7:14 says *"If my people, which are called by my name, shall humble themselves and pray, seek my face, and turn from their wicked ways: then I will hear from heaven, and will forgive their sin, and will heal their land."* In every major city there are certain freeways that will take you to certain places. Our lives are like freeways that take us to different areas. There are signs and warnings along the way. If we are to travel the same road we will reach the same destination. In the Dallas-Ft. Worth metroplex, there are roads you can take that will only lead you in circles. If you take Loop 12 you will go around the city of Dallas and still end up where you started. It's the same with Loop 820 in Ft. Worth. Many people are on a Loop 12 in their walk with God. They are right at the city but don't know how to enter. They keep taking the wrong exit so they never reach their desired destination. The scripture in *2 Chronicles 7:14* lets us know we need to exit on humility avenue, take a right on prayer, from there start seeking God's face, turn from our wickedness, and we will be at our destination. God said he will do three things:

1. Hear from Heaven - When we pray we want to make sure God hears us. We must keep an open line free from sin.

2. Forgive Sin - When we humble ourselves and pray, He will always forgive.

3. Heal - Whenever there is forgiveness there is always healing that follows.

To better understand how to break the cycle in our lives, we can study the story of Saul and David in 1 Samuel. Saul's continual rebellion held him in a cycle that eventually caused him to be rejected by God. When God rejected Saul, he told Samuel to anoint David. David was anointed to be king before he became king. So therefore Saul had position without power. Look at the contrasts between the life of Saul and of David:

Saul was handsome, well built, popular, and strong, but he killed no giants. David was a ruddy young child who wasn't recognized by anyone until he killed the giant.

Saul was oppressed by evil spirits. David used his gift to bring deliverance. Saul sought to kill David. David protected Saul. Saul sought someone to kill his giant. David killed the giant. Saul made excuses for his sin. David repented for his sin.

To be like a David, you have to have courage to fight your giant, humility to forgive your Saul, faith to overcome your loss, and conviction to repent for your wrong. When you have a repenting heart and a mind to change, there is nothing that can keep you in the cycle. You will be free to reach out to others who are in their cycles.

Gaining Record Breaking Victory from Past Mistakes

Mistakes are defined as an error in action or opinion, or judgement caused by poor reasoning, carelessness, or insufficient knowledge. This is part of our human frailty. Anyone who ever does anything, shall make mistakes. Mistakes can be used as one of the most valuable tools in our growth. In order for mistakes to be beneficial, there are three basic things we must gain from them:

1. Experience

The experience of error should enhance our quest for success. Since experience is the best teacher, why don't we learn? A person's worth is increased by experience. It is something no one can ever take away. It is one of the most personal attributes I have. When all else fails, I have experience to stand on. It reminds me of when I worked for a large aluminum corporation. The company didn't want outside men to come in and handle the plant's maintenance so they made an investment in their own employees. They chose potential laborers and paid for their training. After several months of classroom training and several weeks of actual on the job training, these men were ready to fulfill any maintenance demands that arose. The experience and training invested in the trainees made them among the companies most valued employees. I believe things God allows us to experience, whether good or bad, is God's investment in us. We learn from our mistakes. God brings people in our path who are faced with the same situation we have experienced. We are then able to encourage them to go another way.

Apostle Eugene Satterwhite Th.D.

2. Knowledge

To benefit from mistakes, you must learn. If you don't learn then suffering is in vain. Lack of knowledge can be the most devastating thing in your life. Life has been lost because of lack of knowledge. How many times have you witnessed a change being instituted after someone died? We gained knowledge about how seat belts can save lives but someone died for that knowledge.

Many inventions were made because of mistakes. As a cook I've created some of my best recipes from what was a mistake. Each bit of knowledge I gained from the mistake makes the recipe better the next time.

The knowledge I gained from past experience has also spared me a lot of pain. I remember when I was out barbequing on my large, iron pit. I failed to secure the latch when I was checking the meat. The pit door came down and hit me in the head. I had to go to the hospital for stitches. I could have easily been killed from the weight of the pit door. The knowledge I gained from this experience will save my life in the future. Every time I've dealt with the pit from that day forth, I first make sure the latch is secure. I will never need to experience that again. Therefore a hospital bill was better than funeral expenses.

When we are suffering from grief and loss, we will make mistakes in the recovery process. It is only a sign that we are still in the race. We haven't given up. This is what I call progress.

3. Humility

It is quite hard to be haughty with arrogance after being humbled with error. When we are riding our cloud of success, mistakes have a way of bringing us back down to earth again. Although much discretion must be used as to who, when, where, and how, as a leader I believe my counsel can often be more effective when I disclose past failures. Many people I've ministered to, especially in the area of grief and loss, were relieved to know I too, had been through failures. If I portray myself as Mr. Perfect many times people will shy away from me thinking I couldn't possibly understand what they are going through. Someone had patience with me, therefore I must be patient with others when they fail or make mistakes. To better help you overcome your mistakes, there are seven 'nevers' of mistakes:

1. Never cover a mistake, correct it.
2. Never excuse a mistake.
3. Never lose hope or stop trying because of a mistake.
4. Never blame others for your mistakes.
5. Never blame God for your mistakes.
6. Never misjudge or take your mistakes too lightly.
7. Never dwell continually on mistakes, move on.

To totally avoid mistakes, you must use past mistakes as a reference. If a mistake happened once, don't let it happen again. Follow the steps of Christ. Be lead by the spirit. He never makes mistakes

To gain record breaking victory. You must realize mistakes are not always sin or failure unless you choose it to be. In the beginning failure came because of sin, sin didn't come because of failure. Therefore, it is sin in our lives we need to deal with. You may not seem to be breaking any record but you are a winner if you stay in the fight. Many times we want to be spectacular and break records by super exceeding all others in the race. However, we should focus on personal battles first. In other words, you can strive to break your own record by being able to say, "I went a whole day without lying, or I went all week without overeating or I didn't gossip at all this month." You may have to overcome one thing at a time, one step at a time. Before you endeavor to do what no one else has ever done, try doing what you have never done. Set yourself some achievable

Apostle Eugene Satterwhite Th.D.

goals and then outline a plan of attack. In setting goals, remember the three "W's" - what, why, and when. What do you want to achieve? Why do you want to achieve it? (People without a reason to pursue their dreams usually never do.) Then you must decide when you want to achieve it. It is important to set reasonable long and short term goals.

Facing Tomorrow

Facing tomorrow can be the greatest challenge for a person suffering from grief and loss. Facing tomorrow is more devastating when you lose someone you are totally dependent on. I've known wives who lost their companion who was their only source of income. The only thing they knew was being a housewife. Their tomorrow was hard to face. There were many times in my life when I wished I could have cancelled tomorrow. I wished I could go to sleep and wake up somewhere in my future and find the hurts and pain of the past were gone forever.

Man's greatest fear is the fear of the unknown. Because we really don't know about tomorrow we often fear it. We don't know what it really holds for us. We don't know what changes will come or how we will adapt to such changes. You can liken tomorrow to a woman. You can't rush her or slow her down. You wait for her although there is no guarantee you will see her. She can be your best friend or worse enemy. She is never the same when she shows up. Sometimes she brings with her sunshine and rain, and sometimes she brings with her heartaches and pain. Sometimes I want to invite her in and other times I want to send her away. Just when you think, "I've got her figured out," she goes and changes. Today is her best friend because everyday is her destiny. Tomorrow can't even exist without her today.

Although we may not know everything about tomorrow, we can better face it if we can get an understanding of certain principles about it. I believe that every child of God has his tomorrow predestined by God. I also believe our predestination by God is based on our willingness to follow his plan. For instance, the Children of Israel were predestined for the Promised Land (Canaan), but only two of the original Isralites over the age of 20 (Joshua and Caleb) made it from Egypt to Canaan. The others were their grandchildren. I recently found out not all the Children of Israel left Egypt after they were freed.

Apostle Eugene Satterwhite Th.D.

I wondered why someone who had been in bondage for so long would reject the freedom they once prayed for. It was the same with the African-American slaves that were freed. After receiving their freedom, some of the slaves still chose to live on the plantations in bondage. Here are five major reasons people choose bondage over freedom. These can be applied naturally and spiritually:

1. Employment

Many of the people loved their jobs. I've witnessed to prostitutes and drug addicts who remain in bondage because they love the money they are making. If they surrendered their lives to Christ, they would have to get a legal job. They don't know they have more to gain than lose. How often do we try to work for what Christ wants to freely give us? I heard a true story about parents who had secretly purposed to buy their son a car if he finished college. They didn't tell him of their plans. They began saving money each month for the new car. Their son finished the first year of college but in the second year he dropped out because he was having trouble with the car he was driving. He decided to work two jobs in order to save enough money to buy the car he wanted. Many times in my life I have had to work overtime to get the things I wanted. Had I submitted to God's plan, I would have freely received all that I needed.

2. Relationships

Many of the Israelites fell in love with their Egyptian masters and therefore didn't want to leave Egypt. Many people have allowed bad associations or relationship to hinder them from reaching their spiritual destiny. They may know they are in an unhealthy relationship but they are afraid to face tomorrow alone.

3. Security

Some hold to the saying, "A bird in hand is better than two in the bush." Some of the Israelites loved the security of Egypt and didn't want to face the unknown. All they had to go on was a promise from Moses. They had been told of a land far away given to them by God to worship Him. The Israelites never had any evidence that such a land existed. When the Israelites reached the Red Sea many of them complained they would have rather been left alone to suffer in Egypt than to die in the wilderness. A promise was not enough to sustain them when they were faced with opposition.

4. Too Weak and Feeble to Break Away

Some people have been dictated to for so long they are frightened by the thought of having to make their own decisions. I've known welfare recipients who were totally dependent on the system. They could never face tomorrow if it meant doing things on their own. I found most people who are dependent on others are very insecure people with low self-esteem. Many dependent people who have suffered a loss are too tearful to face tomorrow. They are afraid of failure so they don't try.

5. Pleasure and Comforts of Egypt

Not all of the children of Israel worked in unbearable conditions in the fields. There were those that worked for officers of the king. They got to enjoy the pleasure and comforts of Egypt while they were serving. The bible says in *Hebrews 11:24-25, "By faith Moses, when he was come to years, refused to be called the son of Pharaoh's daughter. Choosing rather to suffer affliction with the people of God than to enjoy the pleasures of sin for a season."*

In these scriptures we find that Moses refused employment, denied relationship status, rejected security and independence,

Apostle Eugene Satterwhite Th.D.

and chose suffering rather than pleasure. When Moses discovered his true identity, he was willing to face his tomorrow even if it had to be faced without the comforts he was accustomed to in Egypt. Remember the first step to the Promised Land is leaving Egypt. Tomorrow's challenge will become victory when we give our hurting hearts to Christ and allow him to pour in the needed courage to face it.

Let There Be Light

"In the beginning God created the heaven and the earth. And the earth was without form and void, and darkness was upon the face of the deep. And the spirit of God moved upon the face of the waters. And God said, "Let there be light, and there was light." Genesis 1:1-3

The reason why I chose this particular scripture is because it reminds me of myself after the death of my loved ones. I wondered if there was light after death. I felt like the earth, void and without form, and darkness was upon my face. I buried myself in a sea of darkness and negativity. When I sought God, His spirit moved on me and said, *"Let there be light."* Light returned in my life. Although there were times I chose not to walk in it, there was light. It is up to me now to take this light to those dark areas in my life and say, let there be light. I have the ability to change the quality of my life. If I am to change the quality of my life I must ask myself, "Am I happy?" If not, why? What would it take to make me happy? Since happiness is a choice, most people think it can be found in money, sex, power, or fame. I have learned these things are only temporal fulfillment for eternal desire. Since we are different in our emotions and desires, what may make one man happy may cause grief to another. We live in a day when more and more people are turning to sexual games of bondage and sadomasochism.

Sadomasochists are those who find great pleasure and fulfillment from pain inflicted on them. Then there are the sadists who get their enjoyment from causing pain to others. Although there are quite a few strange fetishes people have adapted, if you ask people what it would take to make them happy, the majority would respond by naming something they don't have. To the homeless man, it would be a home. To the single person, a companion. The poor would ask for riches. The unemployed would ask for a job. The blind would ask for sight and so on. If the things we don't have, such as money, are the

Apostle Eugene Satterwhite Th.D.

things we think will bring us happiness, then why are there more rich people committing suicide? I believe you can change the quality of your life by just changing your attitude to praise. I define praise as an attitude of gratitude that will enhance my aptitude and lead me to a higher altitude.

You will gain happiness by being grateful for what you do have. You may have the home, the job, the companion, the good health, or riches others feel it would take to make them happy. I know it is true when they say, "You don't really learn to appreciate people or certain things until they are gone." I have learned how to use my losses as a leverage to help me to better appreciate the things that remain. As long as there is life in my body, I can find something I can be thankful for. If I'm thankful, I'm happy.

"Although the fig tree shall not blossom, neither shall fruit be in the vines, the labor of the olive shall fail, and the field shall yield no meat, the flock will be cut off from the fold, and there be no herd in the stalls; Yet I will rejoice in the Lord, I will have joy in the God of my salvation. The Lord is my strength, and he will make my feet like hind feet and he will make me to walk upon high places." Habakkuk 3:17-19.

This is one of my favorite scriptures in the bible. The writer is saying, "No matter what happens in my life, I choose to be happy and rejoice in the Lord." The symbolism of this passage should not be overlooked. The fig tree represents prosperity. The grapes stand for blessings. The yield of the crop meant economic prosperity. When the field produced no food, people would starve to death. No sheep or cattle in the stall meant no control over animals. The author furthur stated every area in his life was threatened but he chose God as a refuge. He had confidence God would be his strength and would make his feet like hind feet. In other words, his feet would be like that of a deer who would be able to leap over every obstacle that got in his way. He would walk on high places like the sure-footed mountain goat. His foot would not slip because it is God who makes him walk.

Today, I can truly say without reservation, I am really happy with life. There are times when I am happy without even trying. Then there are days that seem dark and gloomy. It is during such dark times I have to really work at being happy and letting the light shine in my life. I take great consolation in knowing that darkness can't put out light, but light can put out darkness. The more darkness that comes in a room the greater the light is manifested. A flashlight will hardly be noticed in a well lit room, but let someone turn out the lights, and the light will be seen by all. I want to be that light that shines in the darkness so men can see me and glorify God who is the source of energy I'm plugged into for strength to keep shining. God wants all his children to get plugged in so he can say, "Let there be light. In your finances, in your marriage, in your health, in your household, and in your grief stricken, hurting hearts, LET THERE BE LIGHT!"

About the Author

Dr. Eugene Satterwhite began his ministry at the tender age of sixteen. Since then he has served in many leadership positions. He is the Founder and Pastor of Shekinah Glory Full Gospel Church and the Founder and President of Lovinac Outreach Fellowship, Inc.

After graduating from Lincoln High School in Tacoma, WA, Dr. Satterwhite attended Tacoma Community College for Journalism and Creative Writing. He also earned a certificate of completion in Cooking and Kitchen Management at Bates Vocational Institution. He attended Bible College at the A. L. Hardy Academy where he received his Doctorate of Ministry and Th.D. degrees.

Dr. Satterwhite is the author of several hundred poems and worship songs that are being sung by many diverse cultures throughout the county. He is known for his dramatic poetry presentations. He has been called the "father of rap" because he adapted the method of preaching through rhyme and rhythm about thirty-five years ago, in a way that the worldly rappers could never reciprocate.